493

D1096146

THE ORIGINAL ORDER OF
SHAKESPEARE'S SONNETS

TO
THOSE
STERN BUT FLATTERING
CRITICS

C.B.
B.B.
AND
P.G.

THE ORIGINAL ORDER OF SHAKESPEARE'S SONNETS

BY

SIR DENYS BRAY

METHUEN & CO. LTD.
36 ESSEX STREET W.C.
LONDON

First Published in 1925

PRINTED IN GREAT BRITAIN

CONTENTS

THE SONNETS

(The starred sonnets belong apparently to a second edition, Introduction pp. 34–41 : the Roman numerals give the Quarto order.)

ADORATION

INVITATION TO MARRIAGE AND ESCAPE FROM MORTALITY IN FATHERHOOD

v

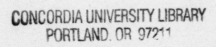
CONCORDIA UNIVERSITY LIBRARY
PORTLAND. OR 97211

TRIUMPH OF LOVE OVER SILENCE AND SEPARATION, OVER THE PASSAGE OF TIME, THE POMPS AND VICISSITUDES OF THE WORLD

REMORSE, CONFESSION, DESPONDENCY AND
FAREWELL

PREFACE

FIRST a word to explain the system I have adopted in the text. Where the rhyme-link, the meaning and function of which are discussed at length in the Introduction, consists in an identical word-link, the word itself is given at the bottom of each of the linked sonnets ; and if there are two or more such words (other than *me* and *thee*, which are not treated as self-sufficient rhyme-links), they are set forth in full. Otherwise the rhyming word or words are enclosed in brackets to emphasize the absence of the normal word-link. For the sake of brevity only one of the two rhymes within the sonnet is given—the rhyme closest to the corresponding rhyme in the linked sonnet. The italicized words represent the links between the sonnets (to which the italicized numerals act as pointers) that join up on the omission of the starred sonnets, which, as explained in the Introduction, are apparently later additions.

I have included T.T.'s Dedication. Properly speaking it has, perhaps, no place outside those editions which follow the order of the Quarto. But whether Mr. W. H. was in fact the Onlie Begetter of the Sonnets in the sense that he was their sole inspiration, or whether, as I fear is more likely, he was the sole filcher of them, it is to Mr. W. H. (for who believes Benson now ?) that we ourselves owe

them.   To Mr. W. H., therefore, be all Happinesse
and that Eternitie promised by our ever-living Poet.

Textual notes have been kept as few as possible.
Two of them are unavoidable, for the emendations
in sonnets 96 and 104 flow directly from the rhyme-
linked sonnet sequence ; slight in themselves—the
substitution of the plural for the singular, the singular
for the plural—they are backed by precedents in
the Quarto.   To the emendations in sonnets 63, 94
and 105, none of which are original, the linked
sequence lends strong support.   In sonnet 35 I have
sought to give new life to an old emendation which
has fallen into unmerited neglect.   In sonnet 51 I
have merely added one more to unnumbered attempts
at enlightening a passage almost certainly corrupt.

I am deeply indebted to Phyllis Gosset for much
fruitful criticism and for godmothering the book
through the press in my absence from England.

D.B.

DELHI,
   Oct. 28, 1924.

INTRODUCTION

TO most lovers of Shakespeare's Sonnets the traditional opening has become so familiar as to render the traditional order of the 1609 Quarto almost sacrosanct. Yet even in the second edition of 1640 irreverent hands were laid on both.

> From fairest creatures we desire increase,
> That thereby beauty's rose might never die,

yielded pride of place to

> Ah, wherefore with infection should he live;
> And with his presence grace impiety?

and difference is hardly less marked than likeness in the rest of the order. Nor did the Quarto order reassert itself readily. True, it was reproduced in the third edition, which appeared in 1710, just a century after the Quarto itself. But it was the 1640 order that was reproduced in the fourth edition, which appeared almost simultaneously; and until nearly the close of the eighteenth century it was the 1640 order that on the whole held sway. From then onwards the Quarto became gradually established as the standard text.

Nevertheless with a quickening of interest in the Sonnets there came a growing dissatisfaction with the traditional order; a growing disbelief, that is, that it represented either the chronological order in which Shakespeare wrote them, or the artistic order in

1

which he finally arranged them; a growing conviction that he had no hand in their publication and that Thorpe, the printer of the 1609 Quarto, had come by them unlawfully and printed them without any sort of authority.

Of the many attempts to reconstruct the true order the first was apparently made by Knight in 1843; rearrangements by Victor Hugo, Cartwright, Bodenstedt, Delius, Massey, Burgersdijk and Stengel followed in rapid succession. Then Dowden's championing of the traditional order stemmed the tide for a while. But only for a while. For the failure of his gallant defence of the continuity of the Sonnets in the Quarto edition will in the end be found to mark a hardening of opinion against the traditional order; the failure of a champion so scholarly, so sane, and so thorough is significant indeed. The tide soon set in again. Few editors, however great their reverence for the Quarto, could refrain from pointing longingly to the apparent linking of this sonnet to that for all their separation in the Quarto; and Copin, von Mauntz, Samuel Butler, Godwin, Stopes and Walsh, came forward one after the other with definite rearrangements of their own. Forrest, who must be almost the latest editor of all, is not content with rearrangement; he allots to the Five Authors of 'Shakes-peare's Sonnets' each his own contribution. Now all these arrangements have a subjective basis. They are based partly on what each editor, often under the stimulus of some splendid or provocative theory, holds to be identity of subject; partly on æsthetics and the like. They are consequently often enough triumphs of literary mosaic. I can lay claim to no such triumph of ingenuity. My own claim is at once greater and more humble. It is no new theory that I have to set forth. Only one hard fact :—the mechanical coupling of sonnet to sonnet by rhyme-link. Nor any brilliant arrangement of my own. Simply Shakespeare's.

Now amidst multitudinous variations, all editors who have attempted to rearrange the Quarto order are agreed on the inseparability of some thirty to forty sonnets found coupled in the Quarto. Nobody, for instance, has ever separated the sonnets which appear as XLIV and XLV in the Quarto, and 36 and 37 in the Text :—

If the dull substance of my flesh were thought,
Injurious distance should not stop my way ;
For then, despite of space, I would be brought,
From limits far remote, where thou dost stay.
No matter then although my foot did stand
Upon the farthest earth remov'd from thee ;
For nimble thought can jump both sea and land,
As soon as think the place where he would be.
But ah, thought kills me, that I am not thought,
To leap large lengths of miles when thou art *gone* ;
But that, so much of earth and water wrought,
I must attend time's leisure with my *moan* ;
 Receiving nought by elements so slow
 But heavy tears, badges of either's woe.

The other two, slight air and purging fire,
Are both with thee, wherever I abide ;
The first my thought, the other my desire,
These present-absent with swift motion slide.
For when these quicker elements are *gone*
In tender embassy of love to thee,
My life, being made of four, with two *alone*
Sinks down to death, oppress'd with melancholy ;
Until life's composition be recur'd
By those swift messengers return'd from thee,
Who even but now come back again, assur'd
Of thy fair health, recounting it to me.
 This told, I joy ; but then no longer glad,
 I send them back again, and straight grow sad.

2

They are linked together inextricably by meaning. Indeed were it not for the first sonnet the second would be unintelligible : only thus can we learn that ' the other two ' make up with ' earth and water' the four elements which constitute ' life's composition '. So wedded are the two that no one, not even the editor of the 1640 edition, has had the hardihood to put them asunder. But now mark —at first sight it will seem a trivial coincidence, possibly even a technical blemish—how common rhymes (*gone–moan* : *gone–alone*, to say nothing for the moment of *thee–be* : *thee–me*) link them mechanically together. Hardly less inseparable is the pair formed by L and LI in the Quarto, 34 and 35 in the text :—

How heavy do I journey on the way,
When what I seek, my weary travel's end,
Doth teach that ease and that repose to say :
' Thus far the miles are measur'd from thy friend ! '
The beast that bears me, tired with my *woe*,
Plods dully on, to bear that weight in me,
As if by some instinct the wretch did *know*
His rider lov'd not speed, being made from thee.
The bloody spur cannot provoke him on
That sometimes anger thrusts into his hide ;
Which heavily he answers with a groan,
More sharp to me than spurring to his side ;
   For that same groan doth put this in my *mind* :
   My grief lies onward, and my joy *behind*.

Thus can my love excuse the slow offence
Of my dull bearer when from thee I speed :
From where thou art why should I haste me thence ?
Till I return, of posting is no need.
O, what excuse will my poor beast then *find*,
When swift extremity can seem but *slow* ?
Then should I spur, though mounted on the *wind*,
In winged speed no motion shall I *know* !

Then can no horse with my desire keep pace ;
Therefore desire, of perfect'st love being made,
Shall weigh no dull flesh in his fiery race ;
But love, for love, thus shall excuse my jade :
  Since from thee going he went wilful-*slow*,
  Towards thee I'll run and give him leave to *go*.

More than a third of the rhymes in these two
sonnets are taken up with mechanical links (*woe–
know*, *mind–behind* in 34 and *slow–know*, *slow–go*,
find–wind in 35) that bind them together. Take
other pairs of sonnets, coupled in the Quarto,
coupled in the second edition, coupled in subsequent
rearrangements, coupled by meaning, and coupled
mechanically by common rhyme. Take, for instance,
29 and 30 which correspond to XLVI and XLVII
in the Quarto :—

Mine eye and heart are at a mortal war,
How to divide the conquest of thy *sight* ;
Mine eye my heart thy picture's sight would bar,
My heart mine eye the freedom of that *right*.
My heart doth plead that thou in him dost lie,
A closet never pierc'd with crystal eyes ;
But the defendant doth that plea deny,
And says in him thy fair appearance lies.
To 'cide this title is impanneled
A quest of thoughts, all tenants to the *heart* ;
And by their verdict is determined
The clear eye's moiety and the dear heart's *part*.
  As thus : mine eye's due is thine outward *part*,
  And my heart's right thine inward love of *heart*.

Betwixt mine eye and heart a league is took,
And each doth good turns now unto the other,
When that mine eye is famish'd for a look,
Or heart in love with sighs himself doth smother.
With my love's picture then my eye doth feast
And to the painted banquet bids my *heart* ;
Another time mine eye is my heart's guest
And in his thoughts of love doth share a *part*.

So, either by thy picture or my love,
Thyself away art present still with me ;
For thou not farther than my thoughts canst move,
And I am still with them and they with thee ;
    Or, if they sleep, thy picture in my *sight*
    Awakes my heart to heart's and eye's *delight*.

The close connection between the two is unmistakable. The mechanical link is as aggressive as
the verbal parallelism. It is a double, almost a
treble link : *sight–right, heart–part, part–heart* in 29,
answering to *sight–delight, heart–part* in 30. But the
examples I have taken may seem too much alike,
conventional and full of conceits at that, lending
themselves to idle repetitions and plays on words. So
let us turn to couples of a very different character.
And again I shall relentlessly quote them in full, for
from the presence of this trivial mechanical link in the
Sonnets flow momentous consequences. Nobody has
ever thought of separating XXXIII and XXXIV,
66 and 67 in the text :—

Full many a glorious morning have I seen
Flatter the mountain-tops with sovereign eye,
Kissing with golden face the meadows green,
Gilding pale streams with heavenly alchemy ;
Anon permit the basest clouds to ride
With ugly rack on his celestial *face*,
And from the forlorn world his visage hide,
Stealing unseen to west with this *disgrace*.
Even so my sun one early morn did shine
With all-triumphant splendour on my brow ;
But, out, alack ! he was but one hour mine,
The region cloud hath mask'd him from me now.
    Yet him for this my love no whit disdaineth ;
    Suns of the world may stain when heaven's sun staineth.

Why didst thou promise such a beauteous day,
And make me travel forth without my cloak,
To let base clouds o'ertake me in my way,
Hiding thy bravery in their rotten smoke ?

'Tis not enough that through the cloud thou break,
To dry the rain on my storm-beaten *face*;
For no man well of such a salve can speak
That heals the wound and cures not the *disgrace*.
Nor can thy shame give physic to my grief;
Though thou repent, yet I have still the loss;
The offender's sorrow lends but weak relief
To him that bears the strong offence's cross.
　Ah, but those tears are pearl which thy love sheds,
　And they are rich and ransom all ill deeds.

Unless the rhyme repetition *face–disgrace* : *face–disgrace* is a purposeful link, it is surely a blemish. Nor has anybody, I think, separated XV and XVI (11 and 12 in the text), linked up by *stay–Decay* : *way–decay* : —

When I consider every thing that grows
Holds in perfection but a little moment,
That this huge stage presenteth nought but shows
Whereon the stars in secret influence comment;
When I perceive that men as plants increase,
Cheered and check'd even by the self-same sky,
Vaunt in their youthful sap, at height decrease,
And wear their brave state out of memory;
Then the conceit of this inconstant *stay*
Sets you most rich in youth before my sight,
Where wasteful Time debateth with *Decay*,
To change your day of youth to sullied night;
　And all in war with Time for love of you,
　As he takes from you, I engraft you new.

But wherefore do not you a mightier *way*
Make war upon this bloody tyrant, Time?
And fortify yourself in your *decay*
With means more blessed than my barren rhyme?
Now stand you on the top of happy hours,
And many maiden gardens, yet unset,
With virtuous wish would bear you living flowers
Much liker than your painted counterfeit.

So should the lines of life that life repair,
Which this time's pencil or my pupil pen,
Neither in inward worth nor outward fair,
Can make you live yourself in eyes of men.
    To give away yourself keeps yourself still;
    And you must live, drawn by your own sweet skill.

Or take I and II (15 and 16), linked up by *eyes–lies*:
lies–eyes :—

From fairest creatures we desire increase,
That thereby beauty's rose might never die,
But as the riper should by time decease,
His tender heir might bear his memory.
But thou, contracted to thine own bright *eyes*,
Feed'st thy light's flame with self-substantial fuel,
Making a famine where abundance *lies*,
Thyself thy foe, to thy sweet self too cruel.
Thou that art now the world's fresh ornament
And only herald to the gaudy spring,
Within thine own bud buriest thy content
And, tender churl, mak'st waste in niggarding.
    Pity the world! or else this glutton be,
    To eat the world's due, by the grave and thee.

When forty winters shall besiege thy brow
And dig deep trenches in thy beauty's field,
Thy youth's proud livery, so gaz'd on now,
Will be a tatter'd weed, of small worth held;
Then being ask'd where all thy beauty *lies*,
Where all the treasure of thy lusty days,
To say, within thine own deep-sunken *eyes*,
Were an all-eating shame and thriftless praise.
How much more praise deserv'd thy beauty's use,
If thou couldst answer ' This fair child of mine
Shall sum my count and make my old excuse,'
Proving his beauty by succession thine!
    This were to be new made when thou art old,
    And see thy blood warm when thou feel'st cold.

Or IX and X (18 and 19), linked up by *behind–mind* :
mind–kind :—

Is it for fear to wet a widow's eye
That thou consum'st thyself in single life?
Ah! if thou issueless shalt hap to die,
The world will wail thee, like a makeless wife.
The world will be thy widow, and still weep
That thou no form of thee hast left *behind*,
When every private widow well may keep
By children's eyes her husband's shape in *mind*,
Look, what an unthrift in the world doth spend
Shifts but his place, for still the world enjoys it;
But beauty's waste hath in the world an end,
And kept unus'd, the user so destroys it.
No love toward others in that bosom sits
  That on himself such murderous shame commits.

For shame deny that thou bear'st love to any,
Who for thyself art so unprovident.
Grant, if thou wilt, thou art belov'd of many,
But that thou none lov'st is most evident;
For thou art so possess'd with murderous hate
That 'gainst thyself thou stick'st not to conspire,
Seeking that beauteous roof to ruinate
Which to repair should be thy chief desire.
O, change thy thought, that I may change my *mind*!
Shall hate be fairer lodg'd than gentle love?
Be, as thy presence is, gracious and *kind*,
Or to thyself at least kind-hearted prove:
  Make thee another self, for love of me,
  That beauty still may live in thine or thee.

Or V and VI (21 and 22), linked up by *on–gone*,
there–where : *loan–one, fair–heir* :—

Those hours that with gentle work did frame
The lovely gaze where every eye doth dwell,
Will play the tyrants to the very same
And that unfair which fairly doth excel.
For never-resting time leads summer *on*
To hideous winter, and confounds him *there*;
Sap check'd with frost and lusty leaves quite *gone*,
Beauty o'ersnow'd and bareness every *where*.

Then, were not summer's distillation left,
A liquid prisoner pent in walls of glass,
Beauty's effect with beauty were bereft,
Nor it, nor no remembrance what it was!
 But flowers distill'd, though they with winter meet,
 Leese but their show : their substance still lives sweet.

Then let not winter's ragged hand deface
In thee thy summer, ere thou be distill'd.
Make sweet some vial ; treasure thou some place
With beauty's treasure, ere it be self-kill'd.
That use is not forbidden usury,
Which happies those that pay the willing *loan* ;
That's for thyself to breed another thee,
Or ten times happier, be it ten for *one* ;
Ten times thyself were happier than thou art,
If ten of thine ten times refigur'd thee ;
Then what could death do, if thou should'st depart,
Leaving thee living in posterity ?
 Be not self-will'd, for thou art much too *fair*
 To be death's conquest and make worms thine *heir*.

Or LXXIII and LXXIV (42 and 43), linked up by *day–away, west–rest* : *away–stay, arrest–interest* :—

That time of year thou mayst in me behold
When yellow leaves, or none, or few, do hang
Upon those boughs which shake against the cold,
Bare ruin'd choirs, where late the sweet birds sang.
In me thou see'st the twilight of such *day*
As after sunset fadeth in the *west* ;
Which by and by black night doth take *away*,
Death's second self, that seals up all in *rest*.
In me thou see'st the glowing of such fire,
That on the ashes of his youth doth lie,
As the death-bed whereon it must expire,
Consum'd with that which it was nourish'd by.
 This thou perceiv'st, which makes thy love more strong,
 To love that well which thou must leave ere long.

But be contented : when that fell *arrest*
Without all bail shall carry me *away*,
My life hath in this line some *interest*,
Which for memorial still with thee shall *stay*.

When thou reviewest this, thou dost review
The very part was consecrate to thee :
The earth can have but earth, which is his due ;
My spirit is thine, the better part of me.
So then thou hast but lost the dregs of life,
The prey of worms, my body being dead ;
The coward conquest of a wretch's knife,
Too base of thee to be remembered.
  The worth of that is that which it contains,
  And that is this, and this with thee remains.

Or LXXXIV, LXXXV and LXXXVI (50, 51 and 52),
linked up by *you–grew* : *true–you* : *you–grew*, with
an additional link *more–store* : *more–before* between
the first two : —

Who is it that says most ? which can say *more*
Than this rich praise, that you alone are *you* ?
In whose confine immured is the *store*
Which should example where your equal *grew*.
Lean penury within that pen doth dwell
That to his subject lends not some small glory ;
But he that writes of you, if he can tell
That you are you, so dignifies his story.
Let him but copy what in you is writ,
Not making worse what nature made so clear,
And such a counterpart shall fame his wit,
Making his style admired every where.
  You to your beauteous blessings add a curse,
  Being fond on praise which makes your praises worse.

My tongue-tied Muse in manners holds her still,
While comments of your praise, richly compil'd,
Rehearsers character with golden quill,
And precious phrase by all the Muses fil'd.
I think good thoughts, whilst other write good words,
And, like unletter'd clerk, still cry ' Amen '
To every hymn that able spirit affords,
In polish'd form of well refined pen.
Hearing you prais'd, I say ' 'Tis so, 'tis *true*,'
And to the most of praise add something *more* ;

But that is in my thought, whose love to *you*,
Though words come hindmost, holds his rank *before*.
    Then others for the breath of words respect,
    Me for my dumb thoughts, speaking in effect.

Was it the proud full sail of his great verse,
Bound for the prize of all too precious *you*,
That did my ripe thoughts in my brain inhearse,
Making their tomb the womb wherein they *grew*?
Was it his spirit, by spirits taught to write
Above a mortal pitch, that struck me dead?
No, neither he, nor his compeers by night
Giving him aid, my verse astonished.
He, nor that affable familiar ghost
Which nightly gulls him with intelligence,
As victors of my silence cannot boast:
I was not sick of any fear from thence.
    But when your countenance fill'd up his line,
    Then lack'd I matter; that enfeebled mine.

Or LXXX and LXXIX (53 and 54), linked up by *away–decay*: *say–pay*:—

O, how I faint when I of you do write,
Knowing a better spirit doth use your name,
And in the praise thereof spends all his might,
To make me tongue-tied, speaking of your fame!
But since your worth, wide as the ocean is,
The humble as the proudest sail doth bear,
My saucy bark, inferior far to his,
On your broad main doth wilfully appear.
Your shallowest help will hold me up afloat,
Whilst he upon your soundless deep doth ride;
Or, being wreck'd, I am a worthless boat,
He of tall building and of goodly pride.
    Then if he thrive and I be cast *away*,
    The worst was this: my love was my *decay*.

Whilst I alone did call upon thy aid,
My verse alone had all thy gentle grace;
But now my gracious numbers are decay'd,
And my sick Muse doth give another place.

I grant, sweet love, thy lovely argument
Deserves the travail of a worthier pen ;
Yet what of thee thy poet doth invent
He robs thee of, and pays it thee again.
He lends thee virtue, and he stole that word
From thy behaviour ; beauty doth he give,
And found it in thy cheek ; he can afford
No praise to thee but what in thee doth live.
   Then thank him not for that which he doth *say*,
   Since what he owes thee thou thyself dost *pay*.

Or LXX and LXIX (62 and 63), linked up by
show–owe : *show–grow* :—

That thou art blam'd shall not be thy defect,
For slander's mark was ever yet the fair ;
The ornament of beauty is suspect,
A crow that flies in heaven's sweetest air.
So thou be good, slander doth but approve
Thy worth the greater, being woo'd of time ;
For canker vice the sweetest buds doth love,
And thou present'st a pure unstained prime.
Thou hast pass'd by the ambush of young days,
Either not assail'd, or victor being charg'd ;
Yet this thy praise cannot be so thy praise,
To tie up envy, evermore enlarg'd :
   If some suspect of ill mask'd not thy *show*,
   Then thou alone kingdoms of hearts shouldst *owe*.

Those parts of thee that the world's eye doth view
Want nothing that the thought of hearts can mend ;
All tongues, the voice of souls, give thee that due,
Uttering bare truth, even so as foes commend.
Thy outward thus with outward praise is crown'd ;
But those same tongues, that give thee so thine own,
In other accents do this praise confound
By seeing farther than the eye hath shown.
They look into the beauty of thy mind,
And that, in guess, they measu by their deeds ;
Then, churls, their thoughts, a   ir eyes were kind,
To thy fair flower add the   f weeds.
   But why thy odour matcheth not thy *show*,
   The soil is this, that thou dost common *grow*.

Or XCV and XCVI (70 and 71), linked up by *sport–
report* : *sport–resort, sort–report* :—

> How sweet and lovely dost thou make the shame
> Which, like a canker in the fragrant rose,
> Doth spot the beauty of thy budding name !
> O, in what sweets dost thou thy sins inclose !
> That tongue that tells the story of thy days,
> Making lascivious comments on thy *sport*,
> Cannot dispraise but in a kind of praise ;
> Naming thy name blesses an ill *report*.
> O, what a mansion have those vices got
> Which for their habitation chose out thee,
> Where beauty's veil doth cover every blot
> And all things turn to fair that eyes can see !
>   Take heed, dear heart, of this large privilege ;
>   The hardest knife ill us'd doth lose his edge.

> Some say, thy fault is youth, some wantonness ;
> Some say, thy grace is youth and gentle *sport* ;
> Both grace and faults are lov'd of more and less :
> Thou mak'st faults graces that to thee *resort*.
> As on the finger of a throned queen
> The basest jewel will be well esteem'd,
> So are those errors that in thee are seen
> To truths translated and for true things deem'd.
> How many lambs might the stern wolf betray,
> If like a lamb he could his looks translate !
> How many gazers mightst thou lead away,
> If thou wouldst use the strength of all thy state !
>   But do not so ; I love thee in such *sort*,
>   As thou being mine, mine is thy good *report*.

Or XCII and XCIII (72 and 74 [1]), linked up by
lie–die : *eye–history* :—

> But do thy worst to steal thyself away,
> For term of life thou art assured mine ;
> And life no longer than thy love will stay,
> For it depends upon that love of thine.

---

[1] The order in the text, 72 and 74, makes it look as if the
two sonnets were separated after all. It will be seen in the
sequel that this is not quite the case.

Then need I not to fear the worst of wrongs,
When in the least of them my life hath end.
I see a better state to me belongs
Than that which on thy humour doth depend.
Thou canst not vex me with inconstant mind,
Since that my life on thy revolt doth *lie*.
O, what a happy title do I find,
Happy to have thy love, happy to *die* !
 But what's so blessed-fair that fears no blot ?
 Thou mayst be false, and yet I know it not.

So shall I live, supposing thou art true,
Like a deceived husband ; so love's face
May still seem love to me, though alter'd new :
Thy looks with me, thy heart in other place.
For there can live no hatred in thine *eye*,
Therefore in that I cannot know thy change.
In many's looks the false heart's *history*
Is writ in moods and frowns and wrinkles strange;
But heaven in thy creation did decree
That in thy face sweet love should ever dwell;
Whate'er thy thoughts or thy heart's workings be,
Thy looks should nothing thence but sweetness tell.
 How like Eve's apple doth thy beauty grow,
 If thy sweet virtue answer not thy show.

Or LXXXVIII and LXXXIX (76 and 77), linked
up by *belong–wrong* : *tongue–wrong* :—

When thou shalt be dispos'd to set me light,
And place my merit in the eye of scorn,
Upon thy side against myself I'll fight,
And prove thee virtuous, though thou art forsworn.
With mine own weakness being best acquainted,
Upon thy part I can set down a story
Of faults conceal'd, wherein I am attainted ;
That thou in losing me shalt win much glory,
And I by this will be a gainer too :
For bending all my loving thoughts on thee,
The injuries that to myself I do,
Doing thee vantage, double-vantage me.
 Such is my love, to thee I so *belong*,
 That for thy right myself will bear all *wrong*.

Say that thou didst forsake me for some fault,
And I will comment upon that offence ;
Speak of my lameness, and I straight will halt,
Against thy reasons making no defence.
Thou canst not, love, disgrace me half so ill,
To set a form upon desired change,
As I'll myself disgrace. Knowing thy will,
I will acquaintance strangle and look strange ;
Be absent from thy walks ; and in my *tongue*
Thy sweet beloved name no more shall dwell,
Lest I, too much profane, should do it *wrong*,
And haply of our old acquaintance tell.
   For thee, against myself I'll vow debate,
   For I must ne'er love him whom thou dost hate.

Or CXIII and CXIV (105 and 106), linked up by *you–untrue* : *you–true* :—

Since I left you, mine eye is in my mind,
And that which governs me to go about
Doth part his function and is partly blind,
Seems seeing, but effectually is out :
For it no form delivers to the heart
Of bird, of flower, or shape, which it doth latch :
Of his quick objects hath the mind no part,
Nor his own vision holds what it doth catch ;
For if it see the rud'st or gentlest sight,
The most sweet favour or deformed'st creature,
The mountain or the sea, the day or night,
The crow or dove, it shapes them to your feature.
   Incapable of more, replete with *you*,
   My most true mind thus makes mine eye *untrue*.

Or whether doth my mind, being crown'd with *you*,
Drink up the monarch's plague, this flattery ?
Or whether shall I say, mine eye saith *true*,
And that your love taught it this alchemy :
To make of monsters and things indigest
Such cherubins as your sweet self resemble,
Creating every bad a perfect best,
As fast as objects to his beams assemble ?

O, 'tis the first ! 'tis flattery in my seeing,
And my great mind most kingly drinks it up !
Mine eye well knows what with his gust is 'greeing,
And to his palate doth prepare the cup.
   If it be poison'd, 'tis the lesser sin
   That mine eye loves it and doth first begin.

Or CXIX and CXVIII (123 and 124), linked up by
true–anew : *true–you* :—

What potions have I drunk of Siren tears,
Distill'd from limbecks foul as hell within,
Applying fears to hopes and hopes to fears,
Still losing when I saw myself to win !
What wretched errors hath my heart committed,
Whilst it hath thought itself so blessed never !
How have mine eyes out of their spheres been fitted,
In the distraction of this madding fever !
O benefit of ill ! now I find *true*
That better is by evil still made better ;
And ruin'd love, when it is built *anew*,
Grows fairer than at first, more strong, far greater.
   So I return rebuk'd to my content,
   And gain by ills thrice more than I have spent,

Like as, to make our appetites more keen
With eager compounds we our palate urge ;
As, to prevent our maladies unseen,
We sicken to shun sickness when we purge ;
Even so, being full of your ne'er-cloying sweetness,
To bitter sauces did I frame my feeding ;
And sick of welfare found a kind of meetness
To be diseas'd, ere that there was true needing.
Thus policy in love, to anticipate
The ills that were not, grew to faults assur'd,
And brought to medicine a healthful state,
Which, rank of goodness, would by ill be cur'd.
   But thence I learn, and find the lesson *true*,
   Drugs poison him that so fell sick of *you*.

And, lest it be still thought that it is only in one
class of sonnets or in one block of sonnets that

Shakespeare employs such mechanical links, let us break new ground and turn to the Dark Lady. Here at last I can safely forbear to quote. The very title sets up echoes of *Will–still* : *still–Will* through sonnet after sonnet.

Is it mere coincidence that there is this rhyme-link in all these sonnet pairs in the Quarto which have ordinarily been kept linked, however much the Quarto order has been otherwise disturbed ? The link is so marked and so insistent that one is tempted to place the burden of proof forthwith on those who refuse to recognize in it any significance at all. But let us put the matter rapidly to the proof ourselves. If the Quarto order is not inviolable and if the rhyme-link is not arbitrary or fortuitous but something deliberate and significant, then it ought to be found in pairs separated by chance or design in the Quarto, but reunited by the common critical consent of those who have endeavoured to reduce the contents of the Quarto to a more orderly sequence. And here the Arden edition will serve our purpose as well as any. For one thing, it is among the most recent of editions ; for another, Knox Pooler, cautious editor though he is, is at pains to suggest a rearrangement where the Quarto order seems to him hopelessly at fault. I open the book almost at random. ' XXIV. Perhaps this Sonnet . . . should be followed by XLVI.' Place them so, and they correspond to 28 and 29 in the text, linked together by the rhyme-links *heart–art, art–heart, lies–eyes* in 28, and *heart–part, part–heart, eyes–lies* in 29 : —

Mine eye hath play'd the painter, and hath stell'd
Thy beauty's form in table of my *heart* ;
My body is the frame wherein 'tis held,
And perspective it is best painter's *art* ;

For through the painter must you see his skill,
To find where your true image pictur'd *lies*,
Which in my bosom's shop is hanging still,
That hath his windows glazed with thine *eyes*.
Now see what good turns eyes for eyes have done :
Mine eyes have drawn thy shape, and thine for me
Are windows to my breast, where-through the sun
Delights to peep, to gaze therein on thee.
  Yet eyes this cunning want to grace their *art* :
  They draw but what they see, know not the *heart*.

Mine eye and heart are at a mortal war.
How to divide the conquest of thy sight ;
Mine eye my heart thy picture's sight would bar,
My heart mine eye the freedom of that right.
My heart doth plead that thou in him dost lie,
A closet never pierc'd with crystal eyes,
But the defendant doth that plea deny,
And says in him thy fair appearance *lies*.
To 'cide this title is impanneled
A quest of thoughts, all tenants to the *heart* ;
And by their verdict is determined
The clear eye's moiety and the dear heart's *part*.
  As thus : mine eye's due is thine outward *part*,
  And my heart's right thine inward love of *heart*.

The next two entries that catch my eye I will
place together. ' XXVII ... Perhaps continued
in XLIII.' ' LXI. Perhaps continuation of XLIII.'
So rearranged, they stand as 38, 39 and 40 in the
text. Henceforth I will refrain from citing the
rhyme-links and let the italics speak for themselves :—

Weary with toil, I haste me to my bed,
The dear repose for limbs with travel tir'd ;
But then begins a journey in my head,
To work my mind, when body's work's expir'd.
For then my thoughts, from far where I abide,
Intend a zealous pilgrimage to *thee*,
And keep my drooping eyelids open wide,
Looking on darkness which the blind do *see* ;

3

Save that my soul's imaginary *sight*
Presents thy shadow to my sightless view,
Which like a jewel hung in ghastly *night*,
Makes black night beauteous and her old face new.
  Lo, thus, by day my limbs, by night my mind,
  For thee and for myself no quiet find.

When most I wink, then do mine eyes best *see*,
For all the day they view things unrespected;
But when I sleep, in dreams they look on *thee*,
And, darkly bright, are bright in dark directed.
Then thou, whose shadow shadows doth make *bright*,
How would thy shadow's form form happy show
To the clear day with thy much clearer *light*,
When to unseeing eyes thy shade shines so!
How would, I say, mine eyes be blessed made
By looking on thee in the living day,
When in dead night thy fair imperfect shade
Through heavy sleep on sightless eyes doth stay!
  All days are nights to see till I see *thee*,
  And nights bright days when dreams do show thee *me*.

Is it thy will thy image should keep open
My heavy eyelids to the weary *night*?
Dost thou desire my slumbers should be broken,
While shadows like to thee do mock my *sight*?
Is it thy spirit that thou send'st from *thee*
So far from home into my deeds to pry,
To find out shames and idle hours in *me*,
The scope and tenour of thy jealousy?
O no! thy love, though much, is not so great;
It is my love that keeps mine eye awake,
Mine own true love that doth my rest defeat,
To play the watchman ever for thy sake.
  For thee watch I whilst thou dost wake elsewhere,
  From me far off, with others all too near.

To proceed with Knox Pooler: 'LII. Perhaps
a continuation of XLVIII.' The rhyme-links are
there; but in actual fact the order in the text
(32 and 33) is the other way round:—

So am I as the rich, whose blessed *key*
Can bring him to his sweet up-locked treasure,
The which he will not every hour *survey*,
For blunting the fine point of seldom pleasure.
Therefore are feasts so solemn and so *rare*,
Since, seldom coming, in the long year set,
Like stones of worth they thinly placed *are*,
Or captain jewels in the carcanet.
So is the time that keeps you as my *chest*,
Or as the wardrobe which the robe doth hide,
To make some special instant special *blest*,
By new unfolding his imprison'd pride.
  Blessed are you, whose worthiness gives scope,
  Being had, to triumph, being lack'd, to hope.

How careful was I, when I took my *way*,
Each trifle under truest bars to thrust,
That to my use it might unused *stay*
From hands of falsehood, in sure wards of trust
But thou, to whom my jewels trifles *are*,
Most worthy comfort, now my greatest grief,
Thou, best of dearest and mine only *care*,
Art left the prey of every vulgar thief.
Thee have I not lock'd up in any *chest*,
Save where thou art not, though I feel thou art,
Within the gentle closure of my *breast*,
From whence at pleasure thou mayst come and part;
  And even thence thou wilt be stol'n, I fear,
  For truth proves thievish for a prize so dear.

Again: 'CVI cf. LIX.'—They stand 99 and 100
in the text:—

When in the chronicle of wasted time
I see descriptions of the fairest wights,
And beauty making beautiful old rhyme
In praise of ladies dead and lovely knights;
Then, in the blazon of sweet beauty's best,
Of hand, of foot, of lip, of eye, of brow,
I see their antique pen would have express'd
Even such a beauty as you master now.

So all their praises are but prophecies
Of this our time, all you prefiguring;
And, for they look'd but with divining eyes,
They had not skill enough your worth to sing;
    For we, which now behold these present *days*,
    Have eyes to wonder, but lack tongues to *praise*.

If there be nothing new, but that which is
Hath been before, how are our brains beguil'd,
Which, labouring for invention, bear amiss
The second burthen of a former child!
O, that record could with a backward look,
Even of five hundred courses of the sun,
Show me your image in some antique book,
Since mind at first in character was done!
That I might see what the old world could say
To this composed wonder of your frame;
Whether we are mended, or whether better they,
Or whether revolution be the same.
    O, sure I am, the wits of former *days*
    To subjects worse have given admiring *praise*.

Again: 'CIX cf. CXVII.' They stand 108 and
109 in the text:—

O never say that I was false of heart,
Though absence seem'd my flame to qualify.
As easy might I from myself depart
As from my soul, which in thy breast doth lie.
That is my home of love: if I have rang'd,
Like him that travels, I return again;
Just to the time, not with the time exchang'd,
So that myself bring water for my stain.
Never believe, though in my nature reign'd
All frailties that besiege all kinds of blood,
That it could so preposterously be stain'd,
To leave for nothing all thy sum of good;
    For nothing this wide universe I *call*,
    Save thou, my rose; in it thou art my *all*.

Accuse me thus: that I have scanted *all*
Wherein I should your great deserts repay;
Forgot upon your dearest love to *call*,
Whereto all bonds do tie me day by day

That I have frequent been with unknown minds,
And given to time your own dear-purchas'd right;
That I have hoisted sail to all the winds
Which should transport me farthest from your sight.
Book both my wilfulness and errors down,
And on just proof surmise accumulate;
Bring me within the level of your frown,
But shoot not at me in your waken'd hate;
  Since my appeal says I did strive to prove
  The constancy and virtue of your love.

Even in the Dark Lady series, which most editors
seem to regard with Mackail as ' a miscellaneous
and disordered appendix,' Knox Pooler recognizes
the essential cohesion of several sonnets. Thus:
' CLII cf. CXLII.'   They are 136 and 137 in the
text : —

In loving thee thou know'st I am forsworn,
But thou art twice forsworn, to me love swearing;
In act thy bed-vow broke, and new faith torn,
In vowing new hate after new love bearing.
But why of two oaths' breach do I accuse thee,
When I break twenty! I am perjur'd most :
For all my vows are oaths but to misuse thee,
And all my honest faith in thee is lost;
For I have sworn deep oaths of thy deep kindness,
Oaths of thy love, thy truth, thy *constancy*;
And, to enlighten thee, gave eyes to blindness,
Or made them swear against the thing they *see*;
  For I have sworn thee fair; more perjured, I,
  To swear against the truth so foul a lie!

Love is my sin, and thy dear virtue hate,
Hate of my sin, grounded on sinful loving.
O, but with mine compare thou thine own state,
And thou shalt find it merits not reproving;
Or if it do, not from those lips of thine,
That have profan'd their scarlet ornaments
And seal'd false bonds of love, as oft as mine
Robb'd others' beds' revenues of their rents.

Be it lawful I love thee, as thou lov'st those
Whom thine eyes woo as mine importune *thee* ;
Root pity in thy heart, that, when it grows,
Thy pity may deserve to pitied *be*.
　　If thou dost seek to have what thou dost hide,
　　By self-example mayst thou be denied !

And again : ' CXLI cf. CXXXVII.' They are 142
and 143 in the text :—

In faith, I do not love thee with mine *eyes*,
For they in thee a thousand errors note ;
But 'tis my heart that loves what they *despise*,
Who, in despite of view, is pleas'd to dote.
Nor are mine ears with thy tongue's tune delighted ;
Nor tender feeling to base touches prone,
Nor taste, nor smell, desire to be invited
To any sensual feast with thee alone ;
But my five wits nor my five senses can
Dissuade one foolish heart from serving *thee*,
Who leaves unsway'd the likeness of a man,
Thy proud heart's slave and vassal wretch to *be*.
　　Only my plague thus far I count my gain,
　　That she that makes me sin awards me pain.

Thou blind fool, Love, what dost thou to mine *eyes*,
That they behold, and see not what they *see* ?
They know what beauty is, see where it *lies*,
Yet what the best is take the worst to *be*.
If eyes, corrupt by over-partial looks,
Be anchor'd in the bay where all men ride,
Why of eyes' falsehood hast thou forged hooks,
Whereto the judgment of my heart is tied ?
Why should my heart think that a several plot
Which my heart knows the wide world's common place ?
Or mine eyes seeing this, say this is not,
To put fair truth upon so foul a face ?
　　In things right true my heart and eyes have err'd,
　　And to this false plague are they now transferr'd.

These examples—six pairs and a group of three—
will perhaps suffice. Their number could easily be

doubled, to say nothing of examples where Knox Pooler, without assigning to a misplaced sonnet a definite place, consigns it to a group which contains the missing link for it. Here and there, to be sure, Knox Pooler (like others before him) is wholly wide of the mark. But his skill in hitting the mark so often with no mechanical aid to guide him, stirs in me the tribute of envy.

But if there is a rhyme-link in sonnet pairs inextricably coupled in the Quarto, and again in pairs and trios separated in the Quarto but coupled by common critical consent, can the rhyme-link stop at that ? If it is really purposeful—and the sonnets in which we have already traced it are a third of the total—it must serve, one would imagine, a larger purpose than the mere linking of individual sonnets into pairs or trios. If it links individuals together, why not a whole chain of them ? This is quickly put to the test. We have only to turn to a fairly well-defined subject like Thoughts in Absence. Nearly all rearrangements include such a group ; indeed there is rather more agreement over its contents than over most. It consists of fourteen sonnets, 28–41. Of the fourteen, I have already cited no less than twelve as coupled in the Quarto or coupled by later editors, all of course coupled mechanically by common rhyme. As for the other two, 31 and 41, nobody is likely to quarrel over their union with the sonnets next to them ; for the links in meaning are almost as solid as the mechanical links themselves. But the mere linking of sonnet to sonnet is no longer enough. The question is whether all the sonnets in the group so link up as to form one continuous chain. The proof stands clear in the text : it is indeed a strong well-matched chain that this sonnet group presents. There is a striking flow and unity of meaning ; the mechanical links that bind sonnet to sonnet are flawless from end to end.

Let us repeat the test in another group, one even more clearly differentiated—the group of sonnets that deal with what the 1640 editor calls An Invitation to Marriage. No selection on our part is needed : they stand massed together, seventeen in all, at the beginning of the Quarto itself. Quotation of so large a group is of course out of the question. For demonstration we must turn again to the best of all proof—the text itself. Rhyme by rhyme, link by link, the seventeen sonnets 11–27 fall into one continuous chain, in which uniformity of theme, wearisome enough in the disjointed repetitions of the Quarto, is transmuted into unity. Take any theme, any episode—Adoration, Jealousy, Reproaches, Remorse, or what you will—and you will find the same. And as sonnet links by rhyme on to sonnet, so theme links on to theme, until in the end Shakespeare's Sonnets fall into two cycles, the one addressed to the Man right fair, the other to the Woman colour'd ill. So they do, of course, in the Quarto. But with what a difference ! In the Quarto one is striving all the time to preserve (or should I say to create ?) a sense of continuous unity. In the text there is in both cycles an easy flow from sonnet to sonnet, from idea to idea, from subject to subject, each cycle forming a chain by itself, well-knit, compact ; a continuous whole ; a unity both in matter and form. Between the two there is a pause that seems too marked to be other than deliberate. For the last sonnet of the Man cycle is written in feminine rhymes, which the first sonnet alone can parallel ; and the opening

sonnet to the Woman is written in eight-syllabled
verse, to which there is no parallel at all.[1] Yet, pause
notwithstanding, the two cycles are firmly interlinked.
The chain is unbroken from end to end. The Sonnets
form one continuous whole, of which the last sonnet
but one states the theme and furnishes the climax :—

> Two loves I have of comfort and despair,
> Which like two spirits do suggest me still :
> The better angel is a man right fair,
> The worser spirit a woman colour'd ill.

It is my misfortune that I am obliged in the text
to hold up the rhyme-links to scrutiny, link by link.
For one thing, they are unattractive in their naked-
ness. Worse still, their prominence prompts a host
of false impressions. It suggests that Shakespeare
must have meant something cryptic or mystic by
them : that he designed them, for instance, to serve
the initiated as a clue to the order of 154 sonnets
scattered broadcast before the vulgar; and so on,
and so on. Such speculations are idle. They spring
from two fallacies : the one, that Shakespeare had
made up his mind from the very outset to conceal
the true order of the Sonnets ; the other, that the
rhyme-link was his own invention. But even though
it were granted for the sake of argument that it was
Shakespeare himself who broke the chain and substituted the Quarto order, it is a very different
assumption that before he sat down to fashion even
the second and third links of the chain he had re-

---

[1] In the final text the pause is more marked than the link.
In Shakespeare's first edition (see below), where sonnet 128
followed immediately on 126, the link was obtrusive : *state-
gate* 125, *estimate-determinate* 126, *state-gait* 128. Neither *gate*
nor *gait* occurs elsewhere among the rhymes ; and in the
Quarto both are spelt *gate*.

solved not to let it go forth unbroken. For this
there is no warrant whatsoever. It runs counter
to all probability. There is nothing in the first
fifty or sixty sonnets too intimate for others to read
in their proper order.

And mark this. So far from the rhyme-link being
the child of Shakespeare's invention, it was a worka-
day convention of the Elizabethan sonnet sequence,
a device commonly employed to heighten the sense
of connection or continuity. To attempt to justify
this statement in full would carry me into a field
of research which is yet unploughed. I must content myself with two illustrations only. In Sidney's
Astrophel and Stella, first published in 1591, the
link is never long absent from the 110 sonnets,
though effectively obscured when used, as it often
is, to bind alternate and not successive sonnets
together. Take, for instance, the opening and the
close of the sequence. Sonnets 1 to 7 are linked
alternately ; sonnets 96 to 107 are linked successively.
An even better illustration is afforded by Daniel's
Delia, which also appeared first in 1591, printed in
the same book as Astrophel and Stella. A rhyme-
link is found in 45 of the 58 sonnets which make
up the final edition, linking them together into five
groups of 2, one of 3, four of 4, two of 5, and one
of 6. Thirteen sonnets only are left unlinked, and
of these some at any rate were linked in one or other
of the many editions that appeared within the first
ten years.

The rhyme-link is in fact so commonplace a convention in the Elizabethan sonnet sequence that it
would have been strange if Shakespeare had gone
out of his way to avoid it altogether. Not that he
followed others blindly in its use. In his search after

unity he put it to a use which, so far as I know, has
no parallel. Whereas others were content to employ
it fitfully to mark and at the same time to enhance
the connection between the sonnets of a group within
the sequence, Shakespeare employed it universally
from one end of the chain to the other, thereby
giving the Sonnets a continuity, a unity, a oneness,
which other sonnet sequences lack.

For those who have already read unity and continuity into the Quarto, there are no great surprises
in the development of the theme. Subjects glide
insensibly into one another so often that a clear-cut
analysis is no easy matter. But the cycle dedicated
to the Youth flows something like this :—Adoration
(1–8) ; Invitation to marriage and escape from
mortality in fatherhood (9–27) ; Thoughts in absence,
longings and broodings (28–41) ; Forebodings of
death, self-depreciation, jealousy of the rival poet
and others (42–61) ; Warnings against the slanders
and contamination of the world (62–65) ; Reproaches
for the breaking of a twofold truth, hers and his ;
forebodings of desertion ; forgiveness (66–79) ;
Triumph of love over silence and separation, over the
passage of time, and the pomps and vicissitudes of
the world (80–101) ; Remorse, confession, despondency and farewell (102–126). The 28 sonnets
that make up the Dark Lady cycle fall into three
movements 127–138, 139–146, 147–151, each beginning but not ending in a calm, with 152–154 as the
finale to the Sonnets as a whole, and hardly need
further grouping. Here the interest and pleasure of
analysis lie rather in the felicitous linking of individual
sonnets and in the escape from the jarring discords
in the Quarto, from which the only escape hitherto
has been a cowardly repudiation of the Shakespearian

authorship of some pleasant trifle, hopelessly misplaced in the Quarto between mighty opposites.

And now reflect how the amazing sonnet-chain
has come to be reconstructed. Others who have
endeavoured to rearrange the 154 links that have
lain for three centuries scattered in the Quarto,
have been free to choose here or choose there as
their fancy took them. How handicapped in com-
parison the man who can only choose a sonnet if
it is linked by rhyme to the sonnet already in his
hand! He is surely like one who tries to grope his
way out of a labyrinth blindfolded and with feet
shackled. The simile is the very negation of the
truth in actual fact. But would it not be truth
itself, if the rhyme-link, instead of being universal,
designed, and purposeful, were casual, fortuitous,
purposeless? Were it simply that, what but a
miracle could have transformed this fortuitous and
purposeless thing into a guide that should lead us
back after three hundred years to the original order
of Shakespeare's Sonnets?

Left entirely to itself the rhyme-link would, of
course, be a sorry guide. For the rhymes are mostly
commonplace, and several combinations are mechanically possible in the case of nearly every sonnet.
Few sonnets unfortunately are at all comparable
with the opening and the close of the cycle addressed
to the Youth, sonnets 1 and 126, which possess no
more than three linkable rhymes between them.
But aids and checks to the rhyme-link are numerous,
and their cumulative influence so effective that the
actual margin of error is small. First and perhaps
best of all checks is the subject-matter. Congruity
of theme or mood is a great sifter-out of mechanically
possible but inherently impossible links. And even

when the group has been cleared of all extraneous matter, the check is still operative within the group itself. For unless the group is so small that the sonnets fall into their proper place in the chain almost of their own accord (as for instance in the opening group of Adoration), this check is constantly at work, safeguarding the association or flow or development of ideas. Sonnet must link naturally to sonnet. The whole chain of rhyme-linked sonnets must be well-matched and well-knit.

Yet another check lies in the very nature of the rhyme-link. Nearly six times out of seven it consists not merely in a common rhyme but in the repetition of the same rhyming word. Turn back to the many sonnets quoted earlier : they include five pairs only in which the link does not contain the repetition of the same word. Or turn to the opening sonnets in the text : in the first twenty the word-link gives place to a mere rhyme-link thrice only. So normal indeed is the identical word-link that throughout the text I have displayed it at the foot of each sonnet, emphasizing its exceptional absence by placing in brackets the rhyming words which have occasionally to supply its place.

Nor is the word-link Shakespeare's invention. It is another commonplace of the Elizabethan sonnet sequence. Of the 16 links in the 19 sonnets cited from the opening and close of Astrophel and Stella, all but three are word-links. There are 28 word-links among the 33 links in Daniel's Delia. In no less than ten sonnets is the link not merely a rhyme-link, not merely a word-link, but a line-link—the last line of a sonnet (in one instance the last line but one) being repeated as the first line of the sonnet that follows. And from this line-link, too rigid to be bearable for long, though much affected by minor Elizabethans, word- and rhyme-links were presumably evolved.

In the word Shakespeare chooses for the link there seems seldom any particular significance. Yet the word has to be substantial : the slight rhyme *me–thee* so frequent inside the sonnet itself, is never employed by itself to bind sonnet and sonnet together, a fact which has led me throughout the text to ignore *me, thee*, in the analysis of both word and rhyme-link. And the rhyme-link must be a sound, straight-forward rhyme : there are no parallels to such false rhymings within the sonnet as *open–broken* in 40, *re-member'd–tender'd* in 111, or *assure ye–cure me* in 118.

But word or rhyme repetitions do not exhaust Shakespeare's devices for linking the sonnets together. Here and there the links are more of the nature of an elaborate texture than of a chain. Perhaps the best illustration of what I mean is furnished again by Thoughts in Absence, 28–41. Except for one single lapse into a simple rhyme-link at 39–40, the word-link persists from the beginning of the group to the end. But over and above this word-link, we find rhyme after rhyme rising in succession like wave after wave and spreading over three or four sonnets before its force is spent. A rhyme wave is started in 28, another in 29, and others in 30, 31, 32, 34 and so on. *Heart–art, art–heart* in 28 is followed by *heart–part, part–heart* in 29, *heart–part* in 30, *art–part* in 33. *Sight–right* in 29 sets up *sight–delight* in 30, *sight–delight* in 31, then disappears only to return towards the close with *sight–night* in 38, *bright–light* in 39, *night–sight* in 40, and *plight–night, bright–night* in 41. In 30 the new theme is *feast–guest*, which sets up *chest–blest* in 32, *chest–*

breast in 33. Then comes *day–away* in 31, with *key–survey* in 32, *way–stay* in 33, *way–say* in 34, *way–stay* in 36, *day–stay* in 39. *Hide–pride* in 32 leads on to *hide–side* in 34, *abide–slide* in 37, *abide–wide* in 38. *Woe–know* in 34 leads on to *slow–know*, *slow–go* in 35, *slow–woe* in 36, *show–so* in 39. Then come lesser rhyme-waves *find–wind*, *gone–moan*, *thee–be*. Even more striking and significant as a unifying link is the carrying over of the pattern (to revert to my original metaphor) into the succeeding group. *Rest–oppressed* in 41, the last Absence sonnet, is taken up in the Jealousy group by *west–rest* in 42, and *arrest–interest* in 43.

There is another pattern—the linking together of every fourth sonnet—woven into the Absence group. But the rhyme-texture is a little uneven and the design is seen to better advantage in the seven sonnets on Death, 42–48, which usher in the Jealousy group. Here every fourth sonnet is linked up in an almost unbroken series of word-links : *lie* 42— *dead* 43—*pen* 44—*cry* 45—*dead* 46—*pen* 47—*lie* 48. The effect of rhyme-texture so close in a group so small on a subject so clearly defined is a very definite enhancement of the sense of unity. Though I cannot detect a rigid system in all this, the deliberate character of the design is unmistakable. This rhyme-texture constitutes in fact another very useful, if only occasional, check.

Both designs are woven into the sixteen sonnets, 139–154, which bring the Dark Lady and indeed the whole sequence to a close. Here the rhyme-wave rolls slowly : *face–grace* 139, *face–disgrace* 140, *face–place* 141, *place–face* 143 ; *eyes–despise* 142, *eyes–lies* 143, *lies–subtleties* 144, *enemies–injuries* 145, *despise–eyes* 146, *lies–eyes* 147 ; *sight–might* 145,

THE
FRANCIS BACON FOUNDATION
INCORPORATED

white–delight 148, *sight–aright* 149, *bright–night* 150, *might–sight* 151. The interlinking of every fourth sonnet (elsewhere usually as intermittent as in the Absence group) is uniform from end to end. And on top of all this there is a persistent rhyme echo (most noticeable perhaps in the Remorse group), which can be hardly other than designed. And nowhere is this echo more marked than in 152, the Lust sonnet, which is made up of rhymes from 138, 140, 144 and 153.

The last check I have to describe is perhaps the most important, certainly the most interesting of all. Now it is five minutes' work to divide the sonnets mechanically into two categories : (*a*) those in which the pronoun of address (allegorical sonnets excluded) is *thou*, and (*b*) the rest. There are eighty-six personal *thou*-sonnets, pure and simple ; to these must be added sonnet 28, a typical *thou*-sonnet into which a couple of *you's* have managed to creep. The rest of the sonnets consist of thirty-four *you*-sonnets ; eight allegorical sonnets addressed to Love or Time or the Muse, all deceptively *thou*-sonnets in form ; seventeen sonnets which are personal in so far as they are written in the first person and descriptive of the friend or the lover in the third person ; three sonnets which are personal only in so far as they are written of the friend ; and two sonnets which are wholly impersonal. Either category may or may not have to be enlarged by the inclusion of one or more of the four sonnets, 3, 61, 103, 110 ; for these are ambiguous in form : though personal, they do not reveal the person—*thou* or *you*—to whom they are addressed.

Now the difference between the eighty-seven *thou*-sonnets and the thirty-four *you*-sonnets proper has long been the subject of speculation. 'The different uses of these pronouns' (I am abridging Alden) 'were first discussed by Goedeke in 1877, later by Dowden, and have been made the starting-point of various interesting discussions, none of which can be said to have reached any result. Dowden's own summary of the facts is as follows: "Sometimes the choice seems to be determined by considerations of euphony, sometimes of rhyme; sometimes intimate affection seems to indicate the use of *you* and respectful homage that of *thou*; but this is by no means invariable. . . . In the sonnets to a mistress *thou* is invariably employed."' As respectful homage is hardly the keynote of the sonnets to the Dark Lady, these conclusions are disappointing enough. Indeed pursued on these lines, attempts to differentiate between the *you* and *thou*-sonnets seem to lead nowhere.

It is different when we turn once more to the mechanics of the sonnets. Let us examine the rhymes again, and this time double rhymes only, and the repetition of the same rhyming word at that. *Heart–part*, *part–heart* in 29, where there is not only a double rhyme but a double repetition of a rhyming word, is an extreme example of the kind. A more normal example is *state–fate*, *state–gate* in 125. Now of such repetitions of the rhyming word within a sonnet there are fifteen examples in the eighty-seven *thou*-sonnets. In the other category —which may conveniently though roughly be called *you*-sonnets after its chief constituent—there are none.[1] This is too big and definite a mechanical

---

[1] There is one half-exception of extraordinary interest. The Passionate Pilgrim (1599) version of sonnet 144 has *young–tongue*, *young–tongue*, where the Quarto has *young–tongue*, *unjust–trust*.

4

differentiation to be brushed aside as negligible. And the same conviction is forced on us surely, when we judge the matter æsthetically. For this repetition of rhyme and especially of the same rhyming word within a sonnet is a technical flaw, even though it is enshrined in such magic of sound and mastery of words as

> When, in disgrace with fortune and men's eyes
> I all alone beweep my outcast state,

or

> Then hate me when thou wilt; if ever, now;
> Now, while the world is bent my deeds to cross.

And when this marked mechanical difference, this serious technical blemish, is found once in every six sonnets in the one category, and is not found at all in the other, then there seems only one conclusion possible, to wit, the two categories are in some way or another essentially different in kind.

I have been at pains to distinguish the two categories in the text : the *thou*-sonnets, being the more numerous by a score, are left unmarked ; the rest are starred. And now note this astonishing fact. Pull away the starred sonnets, and the *thou*-sonnets (reinforced by sonnet 3, one of the four ambiguous sonnets which defy purely mechanical classification) link up again at once into a continuous, well-knit chain.

So much for the fact. Let me try to give some idea of its implications and powerful influence as a check on the order of the sonnets. A single example ought to bring out what it means. Sonnet 97 will do as well as any. It is a *thou*-sonnet, severed from its fellows by *you*-sonnets on either side of it. If it is really set in its right place, it must of course link up in meaning both with the two nearest *thou*-

sonnets and also with the two *you*-sonnets which stand next to it—unless, to be sure, there is a change of subject : here there happens to be none.   Mechanically the links must be no less complete.   So they are : and they are no mere rhyme-links either, but identical   word-links   throughout.   With   92,   the nearest *thou*-sonnet before it, the links are *soul–control* and *spent* ; with 101, the nearest *thou*-sonnet behind it, *age* ; with 96, the *you*-sonnet in front of it, *time* ; with 98, the *you*-sonnet that follows it, *doom* and *time–rhyme*. Put the matter in term of rhyming words. Of the fourteen rhyming words in sonnet 97 no less than half are repetitions of rhyming words in the four sonnets with which it links up. Put it in terms of rhymes. Of the seven rhymes in sonnet 97 two only are peculiar to itself ; the rest are echoes of rhymes in the four linked sonnets. And though sonnet 97 is an unusually elaborate example, the principle is the same throughout the sonnet chain.   Every *thou*-sonnet links up in meaning and also mechanically with the two nearest *thou*-sonnets, and with any *you*-sonnet that stands immediately next to it. And what follows from this ? You can detach every *you*-sonnet from the chain, and the chain links up again at once, shortened to be sure and less elaborate, here and there perhaps a little abrupt or a trifle obscure in the transition from thought to thought or from mood to mood, but mechanically as perfect and as strong a chain as the larger one from which it has seemingly been fashioned.

And the explanation ?   In a work which is devoted to the exposition of one solid fact and of the great conclusion that follows from it, I hardly like to set forth what must at first seem theory, nothing more

But let us again marshal the facts that have to be accounted for : —

(i) The personal *thou*-sonnets fall, quite mechanically, into a group apart.

(ii) The mechanical differentiation between the *thou*-sonnets and the *you*-sonnets proper (there has not been the same curiosity over the rest of the group) is so startling that editor after editor has sought to discover its meaning.

(iii) More than 17 per cent. of the *thou*-sonnets show yet another mechanical characteristic which is wholly lacking in the other group.

So far as we have got, there is warrant for holding that so marked a mechanical difference between the two groups into which the sonnets are divisible almost as mechanically as a pack of cards into suits, constitutes a difference in kind. And one seems driven into some such working hypothesis as this. The two groups are either the work of different men or the work of the same man at different periods. The rhyme-linked sonnet-chain puts the first alternative (for most of us at any rate) finally out of court. The second alternative is not to be shaken off so easily. On the contrary, it becomes more and more insistent as we continue to marshal the facts for which we have to account : —

(iv) The mechanical characteristic of the *thou*-sonnets is a serious technical blemish. The working hypothesis seems to force itself upon us now in an even more concrete form : the *thou*-sonnets are Shakespeare's earlier, the other sonnets Shakespeare's later and more mature work. This is a large hypothesis indeed, one not to be accepted without many searchings of mind. But is there any other that will cover the puzzling facts as fully ? And is there any other that will cover the last and crowning fact : —

(v) The *thou*-sonnets if extracted from the sonnet-chain without disarrangement of their order link together forthwith to form a harmonious chain by themselves.

An astonishing climax this. In the face of it can one really refuse to entertain the second alternative as a working hypothesis, until another is found— if in truth another ever can be found—to cover the whole body of facts if not better at least as well ? For myself scepticism has been gradually overborne in the tests to which the hypothesis has been put in the working out of the sonnet order, and I now accept it as a fact.

If then it be a fact, how is it to be accounted for ? Something like this, I imagine. Shakespeare wrote the eighty-eight [1] *thou*-sonnets first, arranging them in the linked order in which they stand in the text, and fashioning them gradually—for they contain distinct signs of the passage of time—into the chain composed of the two sonnet cycles addressed to the Youth and the Dark Lady. Then he let his work lie untouched for some time ; long enough at any rate for him unconsciously to discard the use of *thou* and to drop naturally into the use of *you* as the pronoun of address when he came to revise his work. Revision perhaps is the wrong word to use. For he left every one of the earlier sonnets standing, and standing in its original order, merely inserting a fresh sonnet or group of sonnets here and there in the chain, sometimes to clear up an obscurity, sometimes to round off an abruptness in transition,

[1] 86 *thou*-sonnets, *plus* the *thou-you*-sonnet 28, *plus* the ambiguous sonnet 3.

sometimes to relieve the monotony of the personal
sonnets by sonnets allegorical or impersonal in form,
sometimes perhaps for the sheer joy of weaving a
new rhyme pattern into the fabric, sometimes of
course to give fresh inspiration play. It is a fascinat-
ing study that a comparative analysis of the contents
of the two editions will open up ; one that promises
to throw light on some of the many controversies
that have raged round the Sonnets.[1] Every real or
imaginary chronological allusion that has been traced
will have to be scrutinized afresh ; for much will
hang on whether it figured in the Sonnets from the
beginning, or entered later on revision. Past literary
judgments will have to come up for review ; and
not all, I fancy, will be found to need so little restate-
ment as Dowden's surmise that sonnets LXIV–
LXXIV—to which the second edition contributed
no less than seven out of eleven—seems to echo
the graver tone of the later plays.

Now if this is at all near the mark, the most
startling feature about it would be that we have the
original eighty-eight sonnets intact. For note this.
If Shakespeare had torn up a *thou*-sonnet on revision
and substituted a fresh sonnet on the same theme
in its place, then unless the rhyme-texture were
very close or the arm of coincidence very long the
chain of *thou*-sonnets would have been broken. On
the part of almost any other author who sat down
to add sixty-six sonnets to a cycle of eighty-eight
sonnets written some time before, this kingly disdain
to blot out a single sonnet—and there are one or
two which jar a little even on idolatry—would be

[1] Note, for instance, that on this showing all *thou*-sonnets
were written before 1599, the year Jaggard printed the *you*-
sonnets 147 and 153 in The Passionate Pilgrim.

hard to believe. I am not sure that it is not characteristic of Shakespeare. Ben Jonson, who ought to
know, evidently thought so. How vividly he puts
it in that passage in ' Timber or Discoveries ' :—
' I remember, the Players have often mentioned it
as an honour to Shakespeare, that in his writing,
(whatsoever he penn'd) hee never blotted out line.
My answer hath beene, would he had blotted a
thousand. Which they thought a malevolent speech.
I had not told posterity this, but for their ignorance,
who choose that circumstance to commend their
friend by, wherein he most faulted ; and to justifie
mine owne candor, for I lov'd the man, and doe honour
his memory (on this side Idolatry) as much as any.
Hee was (indeed) honest, and of an open, and free
nature, had an excellent Phantoie ; brave notions,
and gentle expressions : wherein hee flow'd with
that facility, that some-time it was necessary he
should be stop'd.'

It is on a wonderful voyage of discovery that the
rhyme-link has led us. Yet how trivial the rhyme-
link is in itself ! And herein lies, I suppose, the
chief reason why it has escaped detection, though
the world has been peering all these years into every
other feature of the Sonnets. Triviality and the
conventional setting in which the rhyme-link seems
embedded in most of the pairs in the Quarto have
been, as it were, its protective colouring. For conventionality seems to settle down on the pairs when
they are torn from the context as they are in the
Quarto, and to crush the vitality out of them. The
pairs which are most inseparable and in which the
rhyme-link is most obvious are among the least
arresting of the sonnets. The mind does not linger
lovingly over them. The plethora of rhyme repeti-

tion and still more of word repetition heightens one's
sense of conventionality and helps to hide the purpose of the rhymes. The very reiteration of the
sounds repels us, and leaves us with the impression
that they are not rhymes at all. But although all this
has helped, I imagine, to keep the secret of their rhyme-
link buried, there has been another influence at work.

> Thou blind fool, Love, what dost thou to mine eyes
> That they behold, and see not what they see ?

Love of the Sonnets, worship of Shakespeare, pious
reverence for the traditional order of the Quarto—
these have been blinding our eyes to what has
stared us in the face.

Was it accident or design that broke the Sonnet-
chain ? Was the orderly disorder of the Quarto
the best an unauthorised publisher could make out
of chaos ; or was it all that Shakespeare—or one
of those friends of his among whom Meres tells us
his ' sugred ' sonnets circulated—intended the world
to possess ? These are puzzling questions. But the
deliberate barrier that is placed in the Quarto between the sonnets to the Youth and the sonnets to
the Dark Lady is significant. To find 154 scattered
sonnets and then to sort them unerringly into the
two groups to which they belong was beyond the
constructive criticism of a casual publisher like the
printer of the Quarto ; I am not sure that it was not
beyond the constructive criticism of any man. Nor
can I believe that the printer came across two separate
groups of scattered sonnets and was able to piece
them together into the seeming orderliness of the
Quarto. Still less likely is it that the chains broke
at haphazard, and that some of the links simply
held together. There is too much method in the

Quarto arrangement for it to be other than the work of design. And if of design, is there any need to look beyond Shakespeare himself ? The motive seems clear enough, at any rate to those of us who have always looked upon the Sonnets as the passionate expression of a storm-swept period in Shakespeare's life. For us there is no difficulty in regarding the orderly disorder of the Quarto as a veil of Shakespeare's own making, to hide or at least to shield his secrets from an ' ill-wresting world.' And, though the withdrawing of the veil has revealed no secrets we did not guess before, has the veil really been transparent all the time ? With others it has surely served Shakespeare's purpose well. For it has mystified many an editor and thousands in their train into reading esoteric mysticism or literary posturing into what is personal and passionately real.

' Hitherto no theory or discovery '—I am quoting the Arden edition—' has increased our enjoyment of any line in the Sonnets or cleared up any difficulty.' Who shall say this now ? Look how the conventional sonnets shed much of their conventionality, become purposeful and ennobled as they return to their rightful place ; how each sonnet over and above its own graciousness takes on a deeper meaning and an added beauty as a living part of the majestic whole. And whose pleasure is not quickened on reading the beloved words anew in the even march of sonnet after sonnet from opening to close, the mind distracted and disturbed no longer, as in the Quarto, by incongruity of idea or mood or subject ? The trivial rhyme-link has restored to the Sonnets that unity which gives a work of art more than half its beauty by giving it almost all its meaning.

I have often wondered whether we should pore so

lovingly over the Sonnets were it not for the mystery
of them.   If all their secrets were laid bare, would
their appeal be so impelling ?   Not quite, I fancy,
at any rate to some of us.   Yet the laying bare of
the well-kept secret of the rhyme-link will rob them
of none of their magic.   Though it will scare many
a brave theory into oblivion, it will leave many
another untouched and set others perhaps astir.   To
the riddle of Fair Youth or Dark Lady or Rival
Poet, it has, for aught I know, no clue to offer.
Though the veil has been lifted ever so little, and
we can now pry upon the Sonnets in the intimacy
in which Shakespeare wrote them, mystery broods
over them still.

TO . THE . ONLIE . BEGETTER . OF
THESE . INSVING . SONNETS .
Mr W. H. ALL . HAPPINESSE .
AND . THAT . ETERNITIE .
PROMISED
BY .
OVR . EVER-LIVING . POET .
WISHETH .
THE . WELL-WISHING .
ADVENTVRER . IN .
SETTING .
FORTH .

T. T.

THE ORIGINAL ORDER
OF SHAKESPEARE'S
SONNETS

I

A WOMAN'S face with Nature's own hand painted
   Hast thou, the master-mistress of my passion ;
A woman's gentle heart, but not acquainted
With shifting change, as is false women's fashion ;
An eye more bright than theirs, less false in rolling,
Gilding the object whereupon it gazeth ;
A maiden hue, all hues in his controlling,
Which steals men's eyes and women's souls amazeth,
And for a woman wert thou first created ;
Till Nature, as she wrought thee, fell a-doting,
And by addition me of thee defeated,
By adding one thing to my purpose nothing.
  But since she prick'd thee out for women's pleasure,
  Mine be thy love, and thy love's use their treasure.

pleasure

2

SOME glory in their birth, some in their skill,
 Some in their wealth, some in their body's force ;
Some in their garments, though new-fangled ill ;
Some in their hawks and hounds, some in their horse ;
And every humour hath his adjunct pleasure,
Wherein it finds a joy above the rest.
But these particulars are not my measure ;
All these I better in one general best :
Thy love is better than high birth to me,
Richer than wealth, prouder than garments' cost,
Of more delight than hawks or horses be ;
And having thee, of all men's pride I boast.
 Wretched in this alone, that thou mayst take
 All this away, and me most wretched make.

pleasure   boast

3

LET those who are in favour with their stars
 Of public honour and proud titles boast,
Whilst I, whom fortune of such triumph bars,
Unlook'd for joy in that I honour most.
Great princes' favourites their fair leaves spread
But as the marigold at the sun's eye,
And in themselves their pride lies buried,
For at a frown they in their glory die.
The painful warrior famoused for fight,
After a thousand victories once foil'd
Is from the book of honour razed quite,
And all the rest forgot for which he toil'd.
 Then happy I, that love and am belov'd
 Where I may not remove nor be remov'd.

boast   eye ; buried

4

THY bosom is endeared with all hearts,
    Which I by lacking have supposed dead;
And there reigns love, and all love's loving parts,
And all those friends which I thought buried.
How many a holy and obsequious tear
Hath dear religious love stol'n from mine eye,
As interest of the dead, which now appear
But things remov'd that hidden in thee lie !
Thou art the grave where buried love doth live,
Hung with the trophies of my lovers gone,
Who all their parts of me to thee did give ;
That due of many now is thine alone.
    Their images I lov'd I view in thee,
    And thou, all they, hast all the all of me.

buried ; eye   appear
                                                eye 6

*5

WHAT is your substance, whereof are you made,
    That millions of strange shadows on you tend ?
Since every one hath, every one, one shade,
And you, but one, can every shadow lend.
Describe Adonis, and the counterfeit
Is poorly imitated after you ;
On Helen's cheek all art of beauty set,
And you in Grecian tires are painted new ;
Speak of the spring and foison of the year,
The one doth shadow of your beauty show,
The other as your bounty doth appear ;
And you in every blessed shape we know.
    In all external grace you have some part,
    But you like none, none you, for constant heart.

appear   part–heart

6

SIN of self-love possesseth all mine eye
And all my soul and all my every part;
And for this sin there is no remedy,
It is so grounded inward in my heart.
Methinks no face so gracious is as mine,
No shape so true, no truth of such account;
And for myself mine own worth do define,
As I all other in all worths surmount.
But when my glass shows me myself indeed,
Beated and chopp'd with tann'd antiquity,
Mine own self-love quite contrary I read;
Self so self-loving were iniquity.
   'Tis thee, myself, that for myself I praise,
   Painting my age with beauty of thy days.

part–heart   heart
4 *eye*

7

MY glass shall not persuade me I am old,
So long as youth and thou are of one date;
But when in thee time's furrows I behold,
Then look I death my days should expiate.
For all that beauty that doth cover thee
Is but the seemly raiment of my heart,
Which in thy breast doth live, as thine in me.
How can I then be elder than thou art?
O, therefore, love, be of thyself so wary
As I, not for myself, but for thee will;
Bearing thy heart, which I will keep so chary
As tender nurse her babe from faring ill.
   Presume not on thy heart when mine is slain;
   Thou gav'st me thine, not to give back again.

heart   date

8

SHALL I compare thee to a summer's day?
  Thou art more lovely and more temperate.
Rough winds do shake the darling buds of May,
And summer's lease hath all too short a date;
Sometime too hot the eye of heaven shines,
And often is his gold complexion dimm'd;
And every fair from fair sometime declines,
By chance or nature's changing course untrimm'd.
But thy eternal summer shall not fade,
Nor lose possession of that fair thou ow'st;
Nor shall Death brag thou wander'st in his shade,
When in eternal lines to time thou grow'st.
  So long as men can breathe, or eyes can see,
  So long lives this, and this gives life to thee!

date   grow'st

9

O THOU, my lovely boy, who in thy power
  Dost hold Time's fickle glass, his sickle, hour;
Who hast by waning grown, and therein show'st
Thy lovers withering as thy sweet self grow'st;
If Nature, sovereign mistress over wrack,
As thou goest onwards, still will pluck thee back,
She keeps thee to this purpose, that her skill
May time disgrace and wretched minutes kill.
Yet fear her, O thou minion of her pleasure;
She may detain, but not still keep, her treasure!
  Her audit, though delay'd, answer'd must be,
  And her quietus is to render thee.

grow'st

                            power; back
                            grow'st 14

5

*10

SINCE brass, nor stone, nor earth, nor boundless
    sea,
But sad mortality o'er-sways their power,
How with this rage shall beauty hold a plea
Whose action is no stronger than a flower?
O, how shall summer's honey breath hold out
Against the wreckful siege of battering days,
When rocks impregnable are not so stout,
Nor gates of steel so strong, but Time decays?
O fearful meditation! where, alack,
Shall Time's best jewel from Time's chest lie hid?
Or what strong hand can hold his swift foot back?
Or who his spoil of beauty can forbid?
    O, none! unless this miracle have might,
    That in black ink my love may still shine bright

power; back   (might)

*11

WHEN I consider every thing that grows
    Holds in perfection but a little moment,
That this huge stage presenteth nought but shows
Whereon the stars in secret influence comment;
When I perceive that men as plants increase,
Cheered and check'd even by the self-same sky,
Vaunt in their youthful sap, at height decrease,
And wear their brave state out of memory;
Then the conceit of this inconstant stay
Sets you most rich in youth before my sight,
Where wasteful Time debateth with Decay,
To change your day of youth to sullied night;
    And all in war with Time for love of you,
    As he takes from you, I engraft you new.

(night)   decay

*12

BUT wherefore do not you a mightier way
    Make war upon this bloody tyrant, Time ?
And fortify yourself in your decay
With means more blessed than my barren rhyme ?
Now stand you on the top of happy hours,
And many maiden gardens, yet unset,
With virtuous wish would bear you living flowers
Much liker than your painted counterfeit.
So should the lines of life that life repair,
Which this time's pencil or my pupil pen,
Neither in inward worth nor outward fair,
Can make you live yourself in eyes of men.
    To give away yourself keeps yourself still ;
    And you must live, drawn by your own sweet skill.

decay

decay

*13

O, THAT you were yourself ! but, love, you are
    No longer yours than you yourself here live.
Against this coming end you should prepare,
And your sweet semblance to some other give.
So should that beauty which you hold in lease
Find no determination ; then you were
Yourself again, after yourself's decease,
When your sweet issue your sweet form should bear.
Who lets so fair a house fall to decay,
Which husbandry in honour might uphold
Against the stormy gusts of winter's day
And barren rage of death's eternal cold ?
    O, none but unthrifts ! dear my love, you know
    You had a father ; let your son say so.

decay

(de)cease ; decay

14

AS fast as thou shalt wane, so fast thou grow'st
  In one of thine, from that which thou departest ;
And that fresh blood which youngly thou bestow'st
Thou mayst call thine when thou from youth con-
  vertest.
Herein lives wisdom, beauty and increase.
Without this, folly, age and cold decay :
If all were minded so, the times should cease
And threescore year would make the world away.
Let those whom Nature hath not made for store,
Harsh, featureless and rude, barrenly perish.
Look, whom she best endow'd she gave the more ;
Which bounteous gift thou shouldst in bounty cherish.
  She carv'd thee for her seal, and meant thereby
  Thou shouldst print more, not let that copy die.

decay ; cease   increase—cease ; die
9 *grow'st*

15

FROM fairest creatures we desire increase,
  That thereby beauty's rose might never die,
But as the riper should by time decease,
His tender heir might bear his memory.
But thou, contracted to thine own bright eyes,
Feed'st thy light's flame with self-substantial fuel,
Making a famine where abundance lies,
Thyself thy foe, to thy sweet self too cruel.
Thou that art now the world's fresh ornament
And only herald to the gaudy spring,
Within thine own bud buriest thy content
And, tender churl, mak'st waste in niggarding.
  Pity the world ! or else this glutton be,
  To eat the world's due, by the grave and thee.

increase—(de)cease ; die   eyes—lies

16

WHEN forty winters shall besiege thy brow
    And dig deep trenches in thy beauty's field,
Thy youth's proud livery, so gaz'd on now,
Will be a tatter'd weed, of small worth held;
Then being ask'd where all thy beauty lies,
Where all the treasure of thy lusty days,
To say, within thine own deep-sunken eyes,
Were an all-eating shame and thriftless praise.
How much more praise deserv'd thy beauty's use,
If thou couldst answer ' This fair child of mine
Shall sum my count and make my old excuse,'
Proving his beauty by succession thine !
    This were to be new made when thou art old,
    And see thy blood warm when thou feel'st it cold.

lies—eyes   use

17

UNTHRIFTY loveliness, why dost thou spend
    Upon thyself thy beauty's legacy ?
Nature's bequest gives nothing, but doth lend,
And being frank, she lends to those are free.
Then, beauteous niggard, why dost thou abuse
The bounteous largess given thee to give ?
Profitless usurer, why dost thou use
So great a sum of sums, yet canst not live ?
For having traffic with thyself alone,
Thou of thyself thy sweet self dost deceive.
Then how, when nature calls thee to be gone,
What acceptable audit canst thou leave ?
    Thy unus'd beauty must be tomb'd with thee,
    Which used, lives th' executor to be.

use   spend

18

IS it for fear to wet a widow's eye
    That thou consum'st thyself in single life ?
Ah ! if thou issueless shalt hap to die,
The world will wail thee, like a makeless wife.
The world will be thy widow and still weep
That thou no form of thee hast left behind,
When every private widow well may keep
By children's eyes her husband's shape in mind.
Look, what an unthrift in the world doth spend
Shifts but his place, for still the world enjoys it ;
But beauty's waste hath in the world an end,
And kept unus'd, the user so destroys it.
    No love towards others in that bosom sits
    That on himself such murderous shame commits.

spend   mind

19

FOR shame deny that thou bear'st love to any,
    Who for thyself art so unprovident.
Grant, if thou wilt, thou art belov'd of many,
But that thou none lov'st is most evident ;
For thou art so possess'd with murderous hate
That 'gainst thyself thou stick'st not to conspire,
Seeking that beauteous roof to ruinate
Which to repair should be thy chief desire.
O, change thy thought, that I may change my mind !
Shall hate be fairer lodg'd than gentle love ?
Be, as thy presence is, gracious and kind,
Or to thyself at least kind-hearted prove :
    Make thee another self, for love of me,
    That beauty still may live in thine or thee.

mind   (hate ;   mind)

20

NOT from the stars do I my judgment pluck,
  And yet methinks I have astronomy ;
But not to tell of good or evil luck,
Of plagues, of dearths, or seasons' quality ;
Nor can I fortune to brief minutes tell,
Pointing to each his thunder, rain and wind,
Or say with princes if it shall go well,
By oft predict that I in heaven find.
But from thine eyes my knowledge I derive,
And, constant stars, in them I read such art,
As truth and beauty shall together thrive,
If from thyself to store thou wouldst convert.
  Or else of thee this I prognosticate :
  Thy end is truth's and beauty's doom and date

(find ; date)   (well)
                                                  art 22

*21

THOSE hours that with gentle work did frame
  The lovely gaze where every eye doth dwell,
Will play the tyrants to the very same
And that unfair which fairly doth excel.
For never-resting time leads summer on
To hideous winter, and confounds him there :
Sap check'd with frost and lusty leaves quite gone,
Beauty o'ersnow'd and bareness every where.
Then, were not summer's distillation left,
A liquid prisoner pent in walls of glass,
Beauty's effect with beauty were bereft,
Nor it, nor no remembrance what it was !
  But flowers distill'd, though they with winter meet,
  Leese but their show : their substance still lives
      sweet.

(dwell)   (there ; gone)

22

THEN let not winter's ragged hand deface
  In thee thy summer, ere thou be distill'd.
Make sweet some vial ; treasure thou some place
With beauty's treasure, ere it be self-kill'd.
That use is not forbidden usury,
Which happies those that pay the willing loan ;
That's for thyself to breed another thee,
Or ten times happier, be it ten for one ;
Ten times thyself were happier than thou art,
If ten of thine ten times refigur'd thee ;
Then what could death do, if thou shouldst depart,
Leaving thee living in posterity ?
  Be not self-will'd, for thou art much too fair
  To be death's conquest and make worms thine heir.

(loan ; fair)   one
20 *art*

23

MUSIC to hear, why hear'st thou music sadly ?
  Sweets with sweets war not, joy delights in joy.
Why lov'st thou that which thou receiv'st not gladly,
Or else receiv'st with pleasure thine annoy ?
If the true concord of well tuned sounds,
By unions married, do offend thine ear,
They do but sweetly chide thee, who confounds
In singleness the parts that thou shouldst bear.
Mark how one string, sweet husband to another,
Strikes each in each by mutual ordering ;
Resembling sire and child and happy mother,
Who, all in one, one pleasing note do sing ;
  Whose speechless song, being many, seeming one,
  Sings this to thee : ' Thou single wilt prove none.'

one   another–mother

24

L OOK in thy glass, and tell the face thou viewest
   Now is the time that face should form another ;
Whose fresh repair if now thou not renewest,
Thou dost beguile the world, unbless some mother.
For where is she so fair whose unear'd womb
Disdains the tillage of thy husbandry ?
Or who is he so fond will be the tomb
Of his self-love, to stop posterity ?
Thou art thy mother's glass, and she in thee
Calls back the lovely April of her prime.
So thou through windows of thine age shalt see,
Despite of wrinkles, this thy golden time.
   But if thou live remember'd not to be,
   Die single, and thine image dies with thee.

another–mother   tomb ; time
                                          prime–time 26

*25

W HO will believe my verse in time to come,
   If it were fill'd with your most high deserts ?
Though yet, heaven knows, it is but as a tomb
Which hides your life and shows not half your parts.
If I could write the beauty of your eyes
And in fresh numbers number all your graces,
The age to come would say ' This poet lies !
Such heavenly touches ne'er touched earthly faces.'
So should my papers, yellow'd with their age,
Be scorn'd, like old men of less truth than tongue,
And your true rights be term'd a poet's rage
And stretched metre of an antique song.
   But were some child of yours alive that time,
   You should live twice : in it and in my rhyme.

tomb ; time   time

26

W HEN I do count the clock that tells the time,
       And see the brave day sunk in hideous night ;
When I behold the violet past prime,
And sable curls all silver'd o'er with white ;
When lofty trees I see barren of leaves,
Which erst from heat did canopy the herd,
And summer's green all girded up in sheaves,
Borne on the bier with white and bristly beard ;
Then of thy beauty do I question make,
That thou among the wastes of time must go,
Since sweets and beauties do themselves forsake
And die as fast as they see others grow ;
       And nothing 'gainst Time's scythe can make de-
            fence—
       Save breed, to brave him when he takes thee hence.

time   (night)
24 *time—prime*

27

L O, in the orient when the gracious light
       Lifts up his burning head, each under eye
Doth homage to his new-appearing sight,
Serving with looks his sacred majesty ;
And having climb'd the steep-up heavenly hill,
Resembling strong youth in his middle age,
Yet mortal looks adore his beauty still,
Attending on his golden pilgrimage ;
But when from highmost pitch, with weary car,
Like feeble age, he reeleth from the day,
The eyes, 'fore duteous, now converted are
From his low tract, and look another way.
       So thou, thyself out-going in thy noon,
       Unlook'd on diest, unless thou get a son.

(light)   still ; son

28

M INE eye hath play'd the painter, and hath
        stell'd
Thy beauty's form in table of my heart;
My body is the frame wherein 'tis held,
And perspective it is best painter's art;
For through the painter must you see his skill,
To find where your true image pictur'd lies,
Which in my bosom's shop is hanging still,
That hath his windows glazed with thine eyes.
Now see what good turns eyes for eyes have done:
Mine eyes have drawn thy shape, and thine for me
Are windows to my breast, where-through the sun
Delights to peep, to gaze therein on thee.
    Yet eyes this cunning want to grace their art:
    They draw but what they see, know not the heart.

still; sun   lies–eyes; heart

29

M INE eye and heart are at a mortal war,
        How to divide the conquest of thy sight;
Mine eye my heart thy picture's sight would bar,
My heart mine eye the freedom of that right.
My heart doth plead that thou in him dost lie,
A closet never pierc'd with crystal eyes;
But the defendant doth that plea deny,
And says in him thy fair appearance lies.
To 'cide this title is impanneled
A quest of thoughts, all tenants to the heart;
And by their verdict is determined
The clear eye's moiety and the dear heart's part.
    As thus: mine eye's due is thine outward part,
    And my heart's right thine inward love of heart.

eyes–lies; heart   sight; heart–part

30

BETWIXT mine eye and heart a league is took,
  And each doth good turns now unto the other ;
When that mine eye is famish'd for a look,
Or heart in love with sighs himself doth smother.
With my love's picture then my eye doth feast
And to the painted banquet bids my heart ;
Another time mine eye is my heart's guest
And in his thoughts of love doth share a part.
So, either by thy picture or my love,
Thyself away art present still with me ;
For thou not farther than my thoughts canst move,
And I am still with them and they with thee ;
  Or, if they sleep, thy picture in my sight
  Awakes my heart to heart's and eye's delight.

heart–part ; sight   took–look ; sight–delight
                                                part 33

*31

SO are you to my thoughts as food to life,
  Or as sweet-season'd showers are to the ground ;
And for the peace of you I hold such strife
As 'twixt a miser and his wealth is found :
Now proud as an enjoyer, and anon
Doubting the filching age will steal his treasure ;
Now counting best to be with you alone,
Then better'd that the world may see my pleasure ;
Sometime all full with feasting on your sight,
And by and by clean starved for a look ;
Possessing or pursuing no delight,
Save what is had or must from you be took.
  Thus do I pine and surfeit day by day,
  Or gluttoning on all, or all away.

sight–delight ; look–took.   treasure–pleasure

*32

SO am I as the rich, whose blessed key
  Can bring him to his sweet up-locked treasure,
The which he will not every hour survey,
For blunting the fine point of seldom pleasure.
Therefore are feasts so solemn and so rare,
Since, seldom coming, in the long year set,
Like stones of worth they thinly placed are,
Or captain jewels in the carcanet.
So is the time that keeps you as my chest,
Or as the wardrobe which the robe doth hide,
To make some special instant special blest,
By new unfolding his imprison'd pride.
  Blessed are you, whose worthiness gives scope,
  Being had, to triumph, being lack'd, to hope.

treasure–pleasure   are ; chest

33

HOW careful was I, when I took my way,
  Each trifle under truest bars to thrust,
That to my use it might unused stay
From hands of falsehood, in sure wards of trust !
But thou, to whom my jewels trifles are,
Most worthy comfort, now my greatest grief,
Thou, best of dearest and mine only care,
Art left the prey of every vulgar thief.
Thee have I not lock'd up in any chest,
Save where thou art not, though I feel thou art
Within the gentle closure of my breast,
From whence at pleasure thou mayst come and part ;
  And even thence thou wilt be stol'n, I fear,
  For truth proves thievish for a prize so dear.

are ; chest   way
30 *part*

34

HOW heavy do I journey on the way,
When what I seek, my weary travel's end,
Doth teach that ease and that repose to say :
' Thus far the miles are measur'd from thy friend ! '
The beast that bears me, tired with my woe,
Plods dully on, to bear that weight in me,
As if by some instinct the wretch did know
His rider lov'd not speed, being made from thee.
The bloody spur cannot provoke him on
That sometimes anger thrusts into his hide ;
Which heavily he answers with a groan,
More sharp to me than spurring to his side ;
  For that same groan doth put this in my mind :
  My grief lies onward, and my joy behind.

way   know

35

THUS can my love excuse the slow offence
Of my dull bearer when from thee I speed :
From where thou art why should I haste me thence ?
Till I return, of posting is no need.
O, what excuse will my poor beast then find,
When swift extremity can seem but slow ?
Then should I spur, though mounted on the wind,
In winged speed no motion shall I know !
Then can no horse with my desire keep pace ;
Therefore desire, of perfect'st love being made,
Shall weigh no dull flesh in his fiery race ;
But love, for love, thus shall excuse my jade :
  Since from thee going he went wilful-slow,
  Towards thee I'll run and give him leave to go.

know   slow

36

IF the dull substance of my flesh were thought,
  Injurious distance should not stop my way;
For then, despite of space, I would be brought,
From limits far remote, where thou dost stay.
No matter then although my foot did stand
Upon the farthest earth remov'd from thee;
For nimble thought can jump both sea and land,
As soon as think the place where he would be.
But ah, thought kills me, that I am not thought,
To leap large lengths of miles when thou art gone;
But that, so much of earth and water wrought,
I must attend time's leisure with my moan;
  Receiving nought by elements so slow
  But heavy tears, badges of either's woe.

slow   gone

37

THE other two, slight air and purging fire,
  Are both with thee, wherever I abide;
The first my thought, the other my desire,
These present-absent with swift motion slide.
For when these quicker elements are gone
In tender embassy of love to thee,
My life, being made of four, with two alone
Sinks down to death, oppress'd with melancholy,
Until life's composition be recur'd
By those swift messengers return'd from thee;
Who even but now come back again, assur'd
Of thy fair health, recounting it to me.
  This told, I joy; but then no longer glad,
  I send them back again, and straight grow sad.

gone   abide

38

WEARY with toil, I haste me to my bed,
     The dear repose for limbs with travel tir'd ;
But then begins a journey in my head,
To work my mind, when body's work's expir'd.
For then my thoughts, from far where I abide,
Intend a zealous pilgrimage to thee,
And keep my drooping eyelids open wide,
Looking on darkness which the blind do see ;
Save that my soul's imaginary sight
Presents thy shadow to my sightless view,
Which like a jewel hung in ghastly night,
Makes black night beauteous and her old face new.
     Lo, thus, by day my limbs, by night my mind,
     For thee and for myself no quiet find.

abide   see

39

WHEN most I wink, then do mine eyes best see,
     For all the day they view things unrespected ;
But when I sleep, in dreams they look on thee,
And, darkly bright, are bright in dark directed.
Then thou, whose shadow shadows doth make bright,
How would thy shadow's form form happy show
To the clear day with thy much clearer light,
When to unseeing eyes thy shade shines so !
How would, I say, mine eyes be blessed made
By looking on thee in the living day,
When in dead night thy fair imperfect shade
Through heavy sleep on sightless eyes doth stay !
     All days are nights to see till I see thee,
     And nights bright days when dreams do show thee
          me.

see   (light)

40

IS it thy will thy image should keep open
My heavy eyelids to the weary night ?
Dost thou desire my slumbers should be broken,
While shadows like to thee do mock my sight ?
Is it thy spirit that thou send'st from thee
So far from home into my deeds to pry,
To find out shames and idle hours in me,
The scope and tenour of thy jealousy ?
O no ! thy love, though much, is not so great,
It is my love that keeps mine eye awake ;
Mine own true love that doth my rest defeat,
To play the watchman ever for thy sake.
  For thee watch I whilst thou dost wake elsewhere,
  From me far off, with others all too near.

(night)   night

41

HOW can I then return in happy plight,
That am debarr'd the benefit of rest ?
When day's oppression is not eas'd by night,
But day by night, and night by day, oppress'd ?
And each, though enemies to either's reign,
Do in consent shake hands to torture me ;
The one by toil, the other to complain
How far I toil, still farther off from thee.
I tell the day to please him, thou art bright
And dost him grace when clouds do blot the heaven ;
So flatter I the swart-complexion'd night :
When sparkling stars twire not thou gild'st the even.
  But day doth daily draw my sorrows longer,
  And night doth nightly make grief's strength seem
    stronger.

night   rest
6

42

THAT time of year thou mayst in me behold
     When yellow leaves, or none, or few, do hang
Upon those boughs which shake against the cold,
Bare ruin'd choirs, where late the sweet birds sang.
In me thou see'st the twilight of such day
As after sunset fadeth in the west ;
Which by and by black night doth take away,
Death's second self, that seals up all in rest.
In me thou see'st the glowing of such fire,
That on the ashes of his youth doth lie,
As the death-bed whereon it must expire,
Consum'd with that which it was nourish'd by.
  This thou perceiv'st, which makes thy love more
      strong,
    To love that well which thou must leave ere long.

rest   away ; rest

43

BUT be contented : when that fell arrest
     Without all bail shall carry me away,
My life hath in this line some interest,
Which for memorial still with thee shall stay.
When thou reviewest this, thou dost review
The very part was consecrate to thee :
The earth can have but earth, which is his due ;
My spirit is thine, the better part of me.
So then thou hast but lost the dregs of life,
The prey of worms, my body being dead ;
The coward conquest of a wretch's knife,
Too base of thee to be remembered.
   The worth of that is that which it contains,
   And that is this, and this with thee remains.

(ar)rest ;   away   dead
                                            (*stay*) 47

*44

OR I shall live your epitaph to make,
　　Or you survive when I in earth am rotten,
From hence your memory death cannot take,
Although in me each part will be forgotten.
Your name from hence immortal life shall have,
Though I, once gone, to all the world must die ;
The earth can yield me but a common grave,
When you entombed in men's eyes shall lie.
Your monument shall be my gentle verse,
Which eyes not yet created shall o'er-read ;
And tongues to be your being shall rehearse.
When all the breathers of this world are dead,
　　You still shall live—such virtue hath my pen—
　　Where breath most breathes, even in the mouths
　　　of men.

dead   (die ; dead)

*45

TIRED with all these, for restful death I cry :
　　As, to behold desert a beggar born,
And needy nothing trimm'd in jollity,
And purest faith unhappily forsworn,
And gilded honour shamefully misplac'd,
And maiden virtue rudely strumpeted,
And right perfection wrongfully disgrac'd,
And strength by limping sway disabled,
And art made tongue-tied by authority,
And folly, doctor-like, controlling skill,
And simple truth miscall'd simplicity,
And captive good attending captain ill.
　　Tir'd with all these, from these would I be gone,
　　Save that, to die, I leave my love alone.

(cry ; strumpeted)   gone

*46

NO longer mourn for me when I am dead
    Than you shall hear the surly sullen bell
Give warning to the world that I am fled
From this vile world, with vilest worms to dwell.
Nay, if you read this line, remember not
The hand that writ it ; for I love you so,
That I in your sweet thoughts would be forgot,
If thinking on me then should make you woe.
O if, I say, you look upon this verse
When I perhaps compounded am with clay,
Do not so much as my poor name rehearse,
But let your love even with my life decay ;
    Lest the wise world should look into your moan,
    And mock you with me after I am gone.

gone   (clay

47

IF thou survive my well-contented day
    When that churl Death my bones with dust shall
        cover,
And shalt by fortune once more re-survey
These poor rude lines of thy deceased lover ;
Compare them with the bettering of the time,
And though they be outstripp'd by every pen,
Reserve them for my love, not for their rhyme,
Exceeded by the height of happier men.
O then vouchsafe me but this loving thought :
' Had my friend's Muse grown with this growing age,
A dearer birth than this his love had brought,
To march in ranks of better equipage.
    But since he died, and poets better prove,
    Theirs for their style I'll read, his for his love.'

(day)   prove–love
43 *(day)*   *pen* 54

*48

O, LEST the world should task you to recite
⠀⠀What merit lived in me, that you should love
After my death, dear love, forget me quite,
For you in me can nothing worthy prove ;
Unless you would devise some virtuous lie,
To do more for me than mine own desert,
And hang more praise upon deceased I
Than niggard truth would willingly impart.
O, lest your true love may seem false in this
That you for love speak well of me untrue,
My name be buried where my body is,
And live no more to shame nor me nor you !
⠀⠀For I am sham'd by that which I bring forth,
⠀⠀And so should you, to love things nothing worth.

love–prove   quite ; forth–worth

*49

A LACK, what poverty my Muse brings forth,
⠀⠀That having such a scope to show her pride,
The argument, all bare, is of more worth
Than when it hath my added praise beside !
O, blame me not, if I no more can write !
Look in your glass, and there appears a face
That over-goes my blunt invention quite,
Dulling my lines and doing me disgrace.
Were it not sinful then, striving to mend,
To mar the subject that before was well ?
For to no other pass my verses tend
Than of your graces and your gifts to tell ;
⠀⠀And more, much more, than in my verse can sit,
⠀⠀Your own glass shows you when you look in it.

forth–worth ; quite   well–tell

*50

WHO is it that says most ? which can say more
     Than this rich praise, that you alone are you ?
In whose confine immured is the store
Which should example where your equal grew.
Lean penury within that pen doth dwell
That to his subject lends not some small glory ;
But he that writes of you, if he can tell
That you are you, so dignifies his story.
Let him but copy what in you is writ,
Not making worse what nature made so clear,
And such a counterpart shall fame his wit,
Making his style admired every where.
    You to your beauteous blessings add a curse,
    Being fond on praise which makes your praises
        worse.

(d)well–tell   more ; you

*51

MY tongue-tied Muse in manners holds her still,
     While comments of your praise, richly com-
         pil'd,
Rehearsers character with golden quill,
And precious phrase by all the Muses fil'd.
I think good thoughts, whilst other write good words,
And, like unletter'd clerk, still cry ' Amen '
To every hymn that able spirit affords,
In polish'd form of well refined pen.
Hearing you prais'd, I say ' 'Tis so, 'tis true,'
And to the most of praise add something more ;
But that is in my thought, whose love to you,
Though words come hindmost, holds his rank before.
    Then others for the breath of words respect,
    Me for my dumb thoughts, speaking in effect.

more ; you   you

*52

WAS it the proud full sail of his great verse,
   Bound for the prize of all too precious you,
That did my ripe thoughts in my brain inhearse,
Making their tomb the womb wherein they grew?
Was it his spirit, by spirits taught to write
Above a mortal pitch, that struck me dead?
No, neither he, nor his compeers by night
Giving him aid, my verse astonished.
He, nor that affable familiar ghost
Which nightly gulls him with intelligence,
As victors of my silence cannot boast;
I was not sick of any fear from thence.
   But when your countenance fill'd up his line,
   Then lack'd I matter; that enfeebled mine.

you   write

*53

O, HOW I faint when I of you do write,
   Knowing a better spirit doth use your name,
And in the praise thereof spends all his might,
To make me tongue-tied, speaking of your fame!
But since your worth, wide as the ocean is,
The humble as the proudest sail doth bear,
My saucy bark, inferior far to his,
On your broad main doth wilfully appear.
Your shallowest help will hold me up afloat,
Whilst he upon your soundless deep doth ride;
Or, being wreck'd, I am a worthless boat,
He of tall building and of goodly pride.
   Then if he thrive and I be cast away,
   The worst was this: my love was my decay.

write   (away)

54

WHILST I alone did call upon thy aid,
 My verse alone had all thy gentle grace ;
But now my gracious numbers are decay'd,
And my sick Muse doth give another place.
I grant, sweet love, thy lovely argument
Deserves the travail of a worthier pen ;
Yet what of thee thy poet doth invent
He robs thee of, and pays it thee again.
He lends thee virtue, and he stole that word
From thy behaviour ; beauty doth he give,
And found it in thy cheek ; he can afford
No praise to thee but what in thee doth live.
 Then thank him not for that which he doth say,
 Since what he owes thee thou thyself dost pay.

(say)   say
47 *pen*   *invent* 58

*55

O TRUANT Muse, what shall be thy amends
 For thy neglect of truth in beauty dyed ?
Both truth and beauty on my love depends ;
So dost thou too, and therein dignified.
Make answer, Muse : wilt thou not haply say,
' Truth needs no colour, with his colour fix'd ;
Beauty no pencil, beauty's truth to lay ;
But best is best, if never intermix'd ? '
Because he needs no praise, wilt thou be dumb ?
Excuse not silence so, for 't lies in thee
To make him much outlive a gilded tomb
And to be prais'd of ages yet to be.
 Then do thy office, Muse ; I teach thee how
 To make him seem long hence as he shows now.

say   dumb–tomb

*56

I NEVER saw that you did painting need,
  And therefore to your fair no painting set ;
I found, or thought I found, you did exceed
The barren tender of a poet's debt ;
And therefore have I slept in your report,
That you yourself, being extant, well might show
How far a modern quill doth come too short,
Speaking of worth, what worth in you doth grow.
This silence for my sin you did impute,
Which shall be most my glory, being dumb ;
For I impair not beauty being mute,
When others would give life and bring a tomb.
  There lives more life in one of your fair eyes
  Than both your poets can in praise devise.

dumb–tomb   show

*57

L ET not my love be call'd idolatry,
  Nor my beloved as an idol show,
Since all alike my songs and praises be
To one, of one, still such, and ever so.
Kind is my love to-day, to-morrow kind,
Still constant in a wondrous excellence ;
Therefore my verse to constancy confin'd,
One thing expressing, leaves out difference.
' Fair, kind, and true,' is all my argument,
' Fair, kind, and true,' varying to other words ;
And in this change is my invention spent,
Three themes in one, which wondrous scope affords.
  ' Fair, kind, and true,' have often liv'd alone,
  Which three till now never kept seat in one.

show   (spent)

58

HOW can my Muse want subject to invent
    While thou dost breathe, that pour'st into my
    verse
Thine own sweet argument, too excellent
For every vulgar paper to rehearse ?
O, give thyself the thanks, if aught in me
Worthy perusal stand against thy sight ;
For who's so dumb that cannot write to thee,
When thou thyself dost give invention light ?
Be thou the tenth Muse, ten times more in worth
Than those old nine which rhymers invocate ;
And he that calls on thee, let him bring forth
Eternal numbers to outlive long date.
    If my slight Muse do please these curious days
    The pain be mine, but thine shall be the praise.

(invent)   verse
54 *invent*

59

SO oft have I invok'd thee for my Muse
    And found such fair assistance in my verse,
As every alien pen hath got my use
And under thee their poesy disperse.
Thine eyes, that taught the dumb on high to sing
And heavy ignorance aloft to fly,
Have added feathers to the learned's wing
And given grace a double majesty.
Yet be most proud of that which I compile,
Whose influence is thine and born of thee ;
In others' works thou dost but mend the style,
And arts with thy sweet graces graced be.
    But thou art all my art, and dost advance
    As high as learning my rude ignorance.

verse   Muse–use

60

I GRANT thou wert not married to my Muse,
And therefore mayst without attaint o'erlook
The dedicated words which writers use
Of their fair subject, blessing every book.
Thou art as fair in knowledge as in hue,
Finding thy worth a limit past my praise ;
And therefore art enforc'd to seek anew
Some fresher stamp of the time-bettering days.
And do so, love ; yet when they have devis'd
What strained touches rhetoric can lend,
Thou truly fair wert truly sympathiz'd
In true plain words by thy true-telling friend,
   And their gross painting might be better us'd
   Where cheeks need blood ; in thee it is abus'd.

Muse–use   Muse–use
                                            praise–days 62

*61

SO is it not with me as with that Muse
Stirr'd by a painted beauty to his verse,
Who heaven itself for ornament doth use
And every fair with his fair doth rehearse ;
Making a couplement of proud compare,
With sun and moon, with earth and sea's rich gems,
With April's first-born flowers, and all things rare
That heaven's air in this huge rondure hems.
O let me, true in love, but truly write,
And then believe me, my love is as fair
As any mother's child, though not so bright
As those gold candles fix'd in heaven's air.
   Let them say more that like of hearsay well ;
   I will not praise that purpose not to sell.

Muse–use   fair–air

62

THAT thou art blam'd shall not be thy defect
    For slander's mark was ever yet the fair ;
The ornament of beauty is suspect,
A crow that flies in heaven's sweetest air.
So thou be good, slander doth but approve
Thy worth the greater, being woo'd of time ;
For canker vice the sweetest buds doth love,
And thou present'st a pure unstained prime.
Thou hast pass'd by the ambush of young days,
Either not assail'd, or victor being charg'd ;
Yet this thy praise cannot be so thy praise,
To tie up envy, evermore enlarg'd.
    If some suspect of ill mask'd not thy show,
    Then thou alone kingdoms of hearts shouldst owe.

fair–air   show
60 *days–praise*

63

THOSE parts of thee that the world's eye doth
    view
Want nothing that the thought of hearts can mend ;
All tongues, the voice of souls, give thee that due,
Uttering bare truth, even so as foes commend.
Thy outward thus with outward praise is crown'd ;
But those same tongues, that give thee so thine own,
In other accents do this praise confound
By seeing farther than the eye hath shown.
They look into the beauty of thy mind,
And that, in guess, they measure by their deeds ;
Then, churls, their thoughts, although their eyes were
    kind,
To thy fair flower add the rank smell of weeds.
    But why thy odour matcheth not thy show,
    The soil is this, that thou dost common grow.

show   (due
                                               deeds 67

*64

A H, wherefore with infection should he live
    And with his presence grace impiety,
That sin by him advantage should achieve
And lace itself with his society ?
Why should false painting imitate his cheek,
And steal dead seeing of his living hue ?
Why should poor beauty indirectly seek
Roses of shadow, since his rose is true ?
Why should he live, now Nature bankrupt is,
Beggar'd of blood to blush through lively veins ?
For she hath no exchequer now but his,
And, proud of many, lives upon his gains.
   O, him she stores, to show what wealth she had
   In days long since, before these last so bad.

(hue)   live

*65

O, HOW much more doth beauty beauteous seem
    By that sweet ornament which truth doth give !
The rose looks fair, but fairer we it deem
For that sweet odour which doth in it live.
The canker-blooms have full as deep a dye
As the perfumed tincture of the roses,
Hang on such thorns, and play as wantonly
When summer's breath their masked buds discloses ;
But, for their virtue only is their show,
They live unwoo'd and unrespected fade ;
Die to themselves. Sweet roses do not so ;
Of their sweet deaths are sweetest odours made.
   And so of you, beauteous and lovely youth,
   When that shall vade, my verse distills your truth.

live   (dye ; show

*66

FULL many a glorious morning have I seen
　Flatter the mountain-tops with sovereign eye,
Kissing with golden face the meadows green,
Gilding pale streams with heavenly alchemy ;
Anon permit the basest clouds to ride
With ugly rack on his celestial face,
And from the forlorn world his visage hide,
Stealing unseen to west with this disgrace.
Even so my sun one early morn did shine
With all-triumphant splendour on my brow ;
But, out, alack ! he was but one hour mine,
The region cloud hath mask'd him from me now.
　Yet him for this my love no whit disdaineth ;
　Suns of the world may stain when heaven's sun
　　staineth.

(eye ; brow)　　　　　　　　　　　　face–disgrace

67

WHY didst thou promise such a beauteous day,
　And make me travel forth without my cloak,
To let base clouds o'ertake me in my way,
Hiding thy bravery in their rotten smoke ?
'Tis not enough that through the cloud thou break,
To dry the rain on my storm-beaten face ;
For no man well of such a salve can speak
That heals the wound and cures not the disgrace.
Nor can thy shame give physic to my grief ;
Though thou repent, yet I have still the loss ;
The offender's sorrow lends but weak relief
To him that bears the strong offence's cross.
　Ah, but those tears are pearl which thy love sheds,
　And they are rich and ransom all ill deeds.

face–disgrace　　　　　　　　　　grief ; loss–cross
63 *deeds*

68

THAT thou hast her, it is not all my grief,
    And yet it may be said I lov'd her dearly ;
That she hath thee, is of my wailing chief,
A loss in love that touches me more nearly.
Loving offenders, thus I will excuse ye :
Thou dost love her, because thou know'st I love her ;
And for my sake even so doth she abuse me,
Suffering my friend for my sake to approve her.
If I lose thee, my loss is my love's gain,
And losing her, my friend hath found that loss ;
Both find each other, and I lose both twain,
And both for my sake lay on me this cross.
    But here's the joy : my friend and I are one ;
    Sweet flattery ! then she loves but me alone.

grief ; loss –cross.   grief

69

TAKE all my loves, my love, yea, take them all ;
    What hast thou then more than thou hadst
       before ?
No love, my love, that thou mayst true love call ;
All mine was thine before thou hadst this more.
Then, if for my love thou my love receivest,
I cannot blame thee for my love thou usest ;
But yet be blam'd, if thou thyself deceivest
By wilful taste of what thyself refusest.
I do forgive thy robbery, gentle thief,
Although thou steal thee all my poverty ;
And yet, love knows, it is a greater grief
To bear love's wrong than hate's known injury.
    Lascivious grace, in whom all ill well shows,
    Kill me with spites ; yet we must not be foes.

grief   (foes)

70

HOW sweet and lovely dost thou make the shame
   Which like a canker in the fragrant rose,
Doth spot the beauty of thy budding name!
O, in what sweets dost thou thy sins inclose!
That tongue that tells the story of thy days,
Making lascivious comments on thy sport,
Cannot dispraise but in a kind of praise;
Naming thy name blesses an ill report.
O, what a mansion have those vices got
Which for their habitation chose out thee,
Where beauty's veil doth cover every blot
And all things turn to fair that eyes can see!
   Take heed, dear heart, of this large privilege;
   The hardest knife ill us'd doth lose his edge.

(rose)   sport–report

71

SOME say, thy fault is youth, some wantonness;
   Some say, thy grace is youth and gentle sport;
Both grace and faults are loved of more and less:
Thou mak'st faults graces that to thee resort.
As on the finger of a throned queen
The basest jewel will be well esteem'd,
So are those errors that in thee are seen
To truths translated and for true things deem'd.
How many lambs might the stern wolf betray,
If like a lamb he could his looks translate!
How many gazers mightst thou lead away,
If thou wouldst use the strength of all thy state!
   But do not so; I love thee in such sort,
   As thou being mine, mine is thy good report.

sport–report   away

72

BUT do thy worst to steal thyself away,
  For term of life thou art assured mine ;
And life no longer than thy love will stay,
For it depends upon that love of thine.
Then need I not to fear the worst of wrongs,
When in the least of them my life hath end ;
I see a better state to me belongs
Than that which on thy humour doth depend.
Thou canst not vex me with inconstant mind,
Since that my life on thy revolt doth lie.
O, what a happy title do I find,
Happy to have thy love, happy to die !
  But what's so blessed-fair that fears no blot ?
  Thou mayst be false, and yet I know it not.

away   (end)
                                         (*lie*) 74

*73

BEING your slave, what should I do but tend
  Upon the hours and times of your desire ?
I have no precious time at all to spend,
Nor services to do, till you require.
Nor dare I chide the world-without-end hour
Whilst I, my sovereign, watch the clock for you,
Nor think the bitterness of absence sour
When you have bid your servant once adieu ;
Nor dare I question with my jealous thought
Where you may be, or your affairs suppose ;
But, like a sad slave, stay and think of nought
Save, where you are how happy you make those.
  So true a fool is love that in your will,
  Though you do any thing, he thinks no ill.

(tend)   (adieu)
  7

74

SO shall I live, supposing thou art true,
 Like a deceived husband ; so love's face
May still seem love to me, though alter'd new :
Thy looks with me, thy heart in other place.
For there can live no hatred in thine eye,
Therefore in that I cannot know thy change.
In many's looks the false heart's history
Is writ in moods and frowns and wrinkles strange ;
But heaven in thy creation did decree
That in thy face sweet love should ever dwell ;
Whate'er thy thoughts or thy heart's workings be,
Thy looks should nothing thence but sweetness tell.
 How like Eve's apple doth thy beauty grow,
 If thy sweet virtue answer not thy show.

(true)   (dwell–tell)
72 (eye)   (true) 76

*75

THAT god forbid that made me first your slave,
 I should in thought control your times of
   pleasure,
Or at your hand the account of hours to crave,
Being your vassal, bound to stay your leisure !
O, let me suffer, being at your beck,
The imprison'd absence of your liberty ;
And patience, tame to sufferance, bide each check,
Without accusing you of injury.
Be where you list : your charter is so strong
That you yourself may privilege your time ;
Do what you will : to you it doth belong
Yourself to pardon of self-doing crime.
 I am to wait, though waiting so be hell,
 Not blame your pleasure, be it ill or well.

(hell–well)   belong

76

WHEN thou shalt be dispos'd to set me light,
  And place my merit in the eye of scorn,
Upon thy side against myself I'll fight,
And prove thee virtuous, though thou art forsworn.
With mine own weakness being best acquainted,
Upon thy part I can set down a story
Of faults conceal'd, wherein I am attainted;
That thou in losing me shalt win much glory,
And I by this will be a gainer too;
For bending all my loving thoughts on thee,
The injuries that to myself I do,
Doing thee vantage, double-vantage me.
  Such is my love, to thee I so belong,
  That for thy right myself will bear all wrong.

belong   wrong
74 (*too*)

77

SAY that thou didst forsake me for some fault,
  And I will comment upon that offence;
Speak of my lameness, and I straight will halt,
Against thy reasons making no defence.
Thou canst not, love, disgrace me half so ill,
To set a form upon desired change,
As I'll myself disgrace; knowing thy will,
I will acquaintance strangle and look strange;
Be absent from thy walks; and in my tongue
Thy sweet beloved name no more shall dwell,
Lest I, too much profane, should do it wrong,
And haply of our old acquaintance tell.
  For thee, against myself I'll vow debate,
  For I must ne'er love him whom thou dost hate.

wrong   hate

78

NO more be griev'd at that which thou hast done :
   Roses have thorns, and silver fountains mud ;
Clouds and eclipses stain both moon and sun,
And loathsome canker lives in sweetest bud.
All men make faults, and even I in this,
Authorizing thy trespass with compare,
Myself corrupting, salving thy amiss,
Excusing thy sins more than thy sins are ;
For to thy sensual fault I bring in sense—
Thy adverse party is thy advocate—
And 'gainst myself a lawful plea commence.
Such civil war is in my love and hate,
   That I an accessary needs must be
   To that sweet thief which sourly robs from me.

hate   sun

79

THOSE pretty wrongs that liberty commits,
   When I am sometime absent from thy heart,
Thy beauty and thy years full well befits,
For still temptation follows where thou art.
Gentle thou art, and therefore to be won,
Beauteous thou art, therefore to be assail'd ;
And when a woman woos, what woman's son
Will sourly leave her till she hath prevail'd ?
Ay me ! but yet thou mightst my seat forbear,
And chide thy beauty and thy straying youth,
Who lead thee in their riot even there
Where thou art forc'd to break a twofold truth :
   Hers, by thy beauty tempting her to thee,
   Thine, by thy beauty being false to me.

son   (there)

80

HOW like a winter hath my absence been
From thee, the pleasure of the fleeting year!
What freezings have I felt, what dark days seen!
What old December's bareness every where!
And yet this time remov'd was summer's time;
The teeming autumn, big with rich increase,
Bearing the wanton burthen of the prime,
Like widow'd wombs after their lord's decease.
Yet this abundant issue seem'd to me
But hope of orphans and unfather'd fruit;
For summer and his pleasures wait on thee,
And, thou away, the very birds are mute;
    Or, if they sing, 'tis with so dull a cheer
    That leaves look pale, dreading the winter's near.

(where)   (where)
                                    (*where*) 89

*81

SWEET Love, renew thy force! Be it not said
Thy edge should blunter be than appetite,
Which but to-day by feeding is allay'd,
To-morrow sharpen'd in his former might.
So, Love, be thou: although to-day thou fill
Thy hungry eyes even till they wink with fulness,
To-morrow see again, and do not kill
The spirit of love with a perpetual dulness.
Let this sad interim like the ocean be
Which parts the shore, where two contracted new
Come daily to the banks, that, when they see
Return of love, more blest may be the view;
    Or call it winter, which, being full of care,
    Makes summer's welcome thrice more wish'd, more
        rare.

(care)   (might; new)

*8₂

FROM you have I been absent in the spring,
    When proud-pied April, dress'd in all his trim,
Hath put a spirit of youth in every thing,
That heavy Saturn laugh'd and leap'd with him.
Yet nor the lay of birds, nor the sweet smell
Of different flowers in odour and in hue,
Could make me any summer's story tell,
Or from their proud lap pluck them where they grew.
Nor did I wonder at the lily's white,
Nor praise the deep vermilion in the rose;
They were but sweet, but figures of delight,
Drawn after you, you pattern of all those!
    Yet seem'd it winter still, and you away,
    As with your shadow I with these did play.

(grew; white)   spring; delight

*8₃

MY love is strengthen'd, though more weak in
    seeming;
I love not less, though less the show appear;
That love is merchandiz'd whose rich esteeming
The owner's tongue doth publish every where.
Our love was new, and then but in the spring,
When I was wont to greet it with my lays;
As Philomel in summer's front doth sing,
And stops her pipe in growth of riper days;
Not that the summer is less pleasant now
Than when her mournful hymns did hush the night;
But that wild music burthens every bough,
And sweets grown common lose their dear delight.
    Therefore, like her, I sometime hold my tongue,
    Because I would not dull you with my song.

spring; delight   every where; (de)light

*84

WHERE art thou, Muse, that thou forget'st so long
To speak of that which gives thee all thy might?
Spend'st thou thy fury on some worthless song,
Darkening thy power to lend base subjects light?
Return, forgetful Muse, and straight redeem
In gentle numbers time so idly spent;
Sing to the ear that doth thy lays esteem
And gives thy pen both skill and argument.
Rise, resty Muse, my love's sweet face survey,
If Time have any wrinkle graven there;
If any, be a satire to decay,
And make Time's spoils despised every where.
  Give my love fame faster than Time wastes life;
  So thou prevent'st his scythe and crooked knife.

every where; light   life–knife

*85

AGAINST my love shall be, as I am now,
With Time's injurious hand crush'd and o'er-worn;
When hours have drain'd his blood and fill'd his brow
With lines and wrinkles; when his youthful morn
Hath travell'd on to age's steepy night,
And all those beauties whereof now he's king
Are vanishing or vanish'd out of sight,
Stealing away the treasure of his spring;
For such a time do I now fortify
Against confounding age's cruel knife,
That he shall never cut from memory
My sweet love's beauty, though my lover's life:
  His beauty shall in these black lines be seen,
  And they shall live, and he in them still green.

life–knife   brow

*86

DEVOURING Time, blunt thou the lion's paws,
  And make the earth devour her own sweet
    brood;
Pluck the keen teeth from the fierce tiger's jaws,
And burn the long-lived phœnix in her blood;
Make glad and sorry seasons as thou fleet'st,
And do whate'er thou wilt, swift-footed Time,
To the wide world and all her fading sweets;
But I forbid thee one most heinous crime:
O, carve not with thy hours my love's fair brow,
Nor draw no lines there with thine antique pen;
Him in thy course untainted do allow
For beauty's pattern to succeeding men.
    Yet do thy worst, old Time! Despite thy wrong,
    My love shall in my verse ever live young.

brow   brow

*87

THUS is his cheek the map of days outworn,
  When beauty liv'd and died as flowers do now,
Before these bastard signs of fair were born,
Or durst inhabit on a living brow;
Before the golden tresses of the dead,
The right of sepulchres, were shorn away,
To live a second life on second head;
Ere beauty's dead fleece made another gay.
In him those holy antique hours are seen,
Without all ornament itself and true,
Making no summer of another's green,
Robbing no old to dress his beauty new;
    And him as for a map doth Nature store,
    To show false Art what beauty was of yore.

brow   dead; seen—green

*88

T O me, fair friend, you never can be old,
    For as you were when first your eye I eyed,
Such seems your beauty still.   Three winters cold
Have from the forests shook three summers' pride,
Three beauteous springs to yellow autumn turn'd
In process of the seasons have I seen,
Three April perfumes in three hot Junes burn'd,
Since first I saw you fresh, which yet are green.
Ah, yet doth beauty, like a dial-hand,
Steal from his figure, and no pace perceiv'd ;
So your sweet hue, which methinks still doth stand,
Hath motion, and mine eye may be deceiv'd.
    For fear of which, hear this, thou age unbred :
    Ere you were born was beauty's summer dead.

seen–green ;   dead   pride ;   stand

89

T HE forward violet thus did I chide :
    Sweet thief, whence didst thou steal thy sweet
        that smells,
If not from my love's breath ?   The purple pride
Which on thy soft cheek for complexion dwells
In my love's veins thou hast too grossly dyed.
The lily I condemned for thy hand,
And buds of marjoram had stol'n thy hair ;
The roses fearfully on thorns did stand,
One blushing shame, another white despair ;
A third, nor red nor white, had stol'n of both,
And to his robbery had annex'd thy breath ;
But, for his theft, in pride of all his growth
A vengeful canker eat him up to death.
    More flowers I noted, yet I none could see
    But sweet or colour it had stol'n from thee.

pride ;   stand   (hair)
80 (hair)

90

THY glass will show thee how thy beauties wear,
　　Thy dial how thy precious minutes waste ;
The vacant leaves thy mind's imprint will bear,
And of this book this learning mayst thou taste :
The wrinkles which thy glass will truly show
Of mouthed graves will give thee memory ;
Thou by thy dial's shady stealth mayst know
Time's thievish progress to eternity ;
Look, what thy memory cannot contain
Commit to these waste blanks, and thou shalt find
Those children nurs'd, deliver'd from thy brain,
To take a new acquaintance of thy mind.
　　These offices, so oft as thou wilt look,
　　Shall profit thee and much enrich thy book.

(wear)　　　　　　　　　　　　　memory–eternity ;　brain

91

THY gift, thy tables, are within my brain
　　Full character'd with lasting memory,
Which shall above that idle rank remain,
Beyond all date, even to eternity :
Or, at the least, so long as brain and heart
Have faculty by nature to subsist ;
Till each to raz'd oblivion yield his part
Of thee, thy record never can be miss'd.
That poor retention could not so much hold,
Nor need I tallies thy dear love to score ;
Therefore to give them from me was I bold,
To trust those tables that receive thee more.
　　To keep an adjunct to remember thee
　　Were to import forgetfulness in me.

brain ;　memory–eternity　　　　　　eternity ;　heart

92

WERE'T aught to me I bore the canopy,
     With my extern the outward honouring?
Or laid great bases for eternity,
Which prove more short than waste or ruining?
Have I not seen dwellers on form and favour
Lose all, and more, by paying too much rent,
For compound sweet forgoing simple savour,
Pitiful thrivers, in their gazing spent?
No, let me be obsequious in thy heart,
And take thou my oblation, poor but free,
Which is not mix'd with seconds, knows no art
But mutual render, only me for thee.
     Hence, thou suborn'd informer! a true soul
     When most impeach'd stands least in thy control.

eternity;   heart   spent
                              spent;   soul-control 97

*93

WHY is my verse so barren of new pride,
     So far from variation or quick change?
Why with the time do I not glance aside
To new-found methods and to compounds strange?
Why write I still all one, ever the same,
And keep invention in a noted weed,
That every word doth almost tell my name,
Showing their birth and where they did proceed?
O, know, sweet love, I always write of you,
And you and love are still my argument;
So all my best is dressing old words new,
Spending again what is already spent;
     For as the sun is daily new and old,
     So is my love still telling what is told.

spent   change–strange;   old–told

*94

NO, Time, thou shalt not boast that I do change !
 Thy pyramids built up with newer might
To me are nothing novel, nothing strange ;
They are but dressings of a former sight.
Our dates are brief, and therefore we admire
What thou dost foist upon us that is old ;
And rather make them born to our desire
Than think that we before have heard them told.
Thy registers and thee I both defy,
Not wondering at the present nor the past,
For thy records and what we see do lie,
Made more or less by thy continual haste.
  This I do vow, and this shall ever be :
  I will be true, despite thy scythe and thee.

change–strange ; old–told   lie

*95

THOSE lines that I before have writ do lie,
 Even those that said I could not love you
dearer.
Yet then my judgment knew no reason why
My most full flame should afterwards burn clearer.
But reckoning Time, whose million'd accidents
Creep in 'twixt vows, and change decrees of kings,
Tan sacred beauty, blunt the sharp'st intents,
Divert strong minds to the course of altering things ;
Alas, why, fearing of Time's tyranny,
Might I not then say ' Now I love you best,'
When I was certain o'er incertainty,
Crowning the present, doubting of the rest ?
  Love is a babe ; then might I not say so,
  To give full growth to that which still doth grow ?

lie   accidents

*96

IF my dear love were but the child of state,
  It might for Fortune's bastard be unfather'd,
As subject to Time's love or to Time's hate,
Weeds among weeds, or flowers with flowers gather'd
No, it was builded far from accidents;
It suffers not in smiling pomp, nor falls
Under the blow of thralled discontents,
Whereto the inviting time our fashion calls.
It fears not policy, that heretic,
Which works on leases of short-number'd hours;
But all alone stands hugely politic,
That it nor grows with heat nor drowns with showers.
  To this I witness call the fools of time,
    Which die for goodness, who have lived for crime.

accidents   time

97

NOT mine own fears, nor the prophetic soul
  Of the wide world dreaming on things to come,
Can yet the lease of my true love control,
Suppos'd as forfeit to a confin'd doom.
The mortal moon hath her eclipse endur'd,
And the sad augurs mock their own presage;
Incertainties now crown themselves assur'd,
And peace proclaims olives of endless age.
Now with the drops of this most balmy time
My love looks fresh, and Death to me subscribes,
Since, spite of him, I'll live in this poor rhyme,
While he insults o'er dull and speechless tribes;
  And thou in this shalt find thy monument,
    When tyrants' crests and tombs of brass are spent.

time   doom; time–rhyme
92 *soul–control; spent*   *age* 101

*98

NOT marble, nor the gilded monuments
    Of princes, shall outlive this powerful rhyme;
But you shall shine more bright in these contents
Than in swept stone, besmear'd with sluttish time.
When wasteful war shall statues overturn,
And broils root out the work of masonry,
Nor Mars his sword nor war's quick fire shall burn
The living record of your memory.
'Gainst death and all-oblivious enmity
Shall you pace forth; your praise shall still find room
Even in the eyes of all posterity
That wear this world out to the ending doom.
   So, till the judgment that yourself arise,
   You live in this, and dwell in lovers' eyes.

rhyme–time; doom   time

*99

WHEN in the chronicle of wasted time
    I see descriptions of the fairest wights,
And beauty making beautiful old rhyme
In praise of ladies dead and lovely knights;
Then, in the blazon of sweet beauty's best,
Of hand, of foot, of lip, of eye, of brow,
I see their antique pen would have express'd
Even such a beauty as you master now.
So all their praises are but prophecies
Of this our time, all you prefiguring;
And, for they look'd but with divining eyes,
They had not skill enough your worth to sing;
    For we, which now behold these present days,
    Have eyes to wonder, but lack tongues to praise.

time   days–praise

*100

IF there be nothing new, but that which is
Hath been before, how are our brains beguil'd,
Which, labouring for invention, bear amiss
The second burthen of a former child!
O, that record could with a backward look,
Even of five hundred courses of the sun,
Show me your image in some antique book,
Since mind at first in character was done!
That I might see what the old world could say
To this composed wonder of your frame;
Whether we are mended, or whether better they,
Or whether revolution be the same.
    O, sure I am, the wits of former days
    To subjects worse have given admiring praise.

days–praise   same

101

WHAT'S in the brain, that ink may character,
Which hath not figur'd to thee my true spirit?
What's new to speak, what new to register,
That may express my love, or thy dear merit?
Nothing, sweet boy! but yet, like prayers divine,
I must each day say o'er the very same;
Counting no old thing old, thou mine, I thine,
Even as when first I hallow'd thy fair name.
So that eternal love in love's fresh case
Weighs not the dust and injury of age,
Nor gives to necessary wrinkles place,
But makes antiquity for aye his page;
    Finding the first conceit of love there bred,
    Where time and outward form would show it dead.

same   thine
97 *age*

102

L ORD of my love, to whom in vassalage
    Thy merit hath my duty strongly knit,
To thee I send this written ambassage,
To witness duty, not to show my wit :
Duty so great, which wit so poor as mine
May make seem bare, in wanting words to show it,
But that I hope some good conceit of thine
In thy soul's thought, all naked, will bestow it ;
Till whatsoever star that guides my moving,
Points on me graciously with fair aspect,
And puts apparel on my tatter'd loving,
To show me worthy of thy sweet respect ;
    Then may I dare to boast how I do love thee !
    Till then not show my head where thou mayst
      prove me.

thine   wit
                                         respect 104

*103

A S an unperfect actor on the stage,
    Who with his fear is put besides his part,
Or some fierce thing replete with too much rage,
Whose strength's abundance weakens his own heart ;
So I, for fear of trust, forget to say
The perfect ceremony of love's rite,
And in mine own love's strength seem to decay,
O'ercharg'd with burthen of mine own love's might.
O, let my books be then the eloquence
And dumb presagers of my speaking breast ;
Who plead for love, and look for recompense,
More than that tongue that more hath more express'd.
    O, learn to read what silent love hath writ !
    To hear with eyes belongs to love's fine wit.

wit   part

104

AGAINST that time, if ever that time come,
      When I shall see thee frown on my defect,
When as thy love hath cast his utmost sum,
Call'd to that audit by advis'd respect ;
Against that time when thou shalt strangely pass,
And scarcely greet me with that sun, thine eye,
When love, converted from the thing it was,
Shall reasons find of settled gravity ;
Against that time do I ensconce me here
Within the knowledge of mine own desert,
And this my hand against myself uprear,
To guard the lawful reasons on thy part :
      To leave poor me thou hast the strength of laws,
      Since why to love I can allege no cause.

part   part
102 *respect*   *part* 108

*105

SINCE I left you, mine eye is in my mind,
      And that which governs me to go about
Doth part his function and is partly blind,
Seems seeing, but effectually is out ;
For it no form delivers to the heart
Of bird, of flower, or shape, which it doth latch :
Of his quick objects hath the mind no part,
Nor his own vision holds what it doth catch ;
For if it see the rud'st or gentlest sight,
The most sweet favour or deformed'st creature,
The mountain or the sea, the day or night,
The crow or dove, it shapes them to your feature.
      Incapable of more, replete with you,
      My most true mind thus makes mine eye untrue.

part   you–(un)true
      8

*106

OR whether doth my mind, being crown'd with
    you,
Drink up the monarch's plague, this flattery?
Or whether shall I say, mine eye saith true,
And that your love taught it this alchemy:
To make of monsters and things indigest
Such cherubins as your sweet self resemble,
Creating every bad a perfect best,
As fast as objects to his beams assemble?
O, 'tis the first! 'tis flattery in my seeing,
And my great mind most kingly drinks it up!
Mine eye well knows what with his gust is 'greeing,
And to his palate doth prepare the cup.
    If it be poison'd, 'tis the lesser sin
    That mine eye loves it and doth first begin.

you–true   seeing

*107

'TIS better to be vile than vile esteem'd,
    When not to be receives reproach of being;
And the just pleasure lost, which is so deem'd
Not by our feeling, but by others' seeing.
For why should others' false adulterate eyes
Give salutation to my sportive blood?
Or on my frailties why are frailer spies,
Which in their wills count bad what I think good?
No, I am that I am, and they that level
At my abuses reckon up their own;
I may be straight, though they themselves be bevel;
By their rank thoughts my deeds must not be shown;
    Unless this general evil they maintain:
    All men are bad and in their badness reign.

seeing   blood–good

THE FRANCIS BACON FOUNDATION

108

O, NEVER say that I was false of heart,
  Though absence seem'd my flame to qualify.
As easy might I from myself depart
As from my soul, which in thy breast doth lie.
That is my home of love : if I have rang'd,
Like him that travels, I return again ;
Just to the time, not with the time exchang'd,
So that myself bring water for my stain.
Never believe, though in my nature reign'd
All frailties that besiege all kinds of blood,
That it could so preposterously be stain'd,
To leave for nothing all thy sum of good ;
  For nothing this wide universe I call,
  Save thou, my rose ; in it thou art my all.

blood–good   call–all
104 (de)part   (stain) 113

*109

ACCUSE me thus : that I have scanted all
  Wherein I should your great deserts repay ;
Forgot upon your dearest love to call,
Whereto all bonds do tie me day by day ;
That I have frequent been with unknown minds,
And given to time your own dear-purchas'd right ;
That I have hoisted sail to all the winds
Which should transport me farthest from your sight.
Book both my wilfulness and errors down,
And on just proof surmise accumulate ;
Bring me within the level of your frown,
But shoot not at me in your waken'd hate ;
  Since my appeal says I did strive to prove
  The constancy and virtue of your love.

all–call   minds ; love

*110

LET me not to the marriage of true minds
　　Admit impediments. Love is not love
Which alters when it alteration finds,
Or bends with the remover to remove.
O, no ! it is an ever-fixed mark,
That looks on tempests and is never shaken ;
It is the star to every wandering bark,
Whose worth's unknown, although his height be taken.
Love's not Time's fool, though rosy lips and cheeks
Within his bending sickle's compass come ;
Love alters not with his brief hours and weeks,
But bears it out even to the edge of doom.
　　If this be error and upon me prov'd,
　　I never writ, nor no man ever lov'd.

minds ; love　　　　　　　　　　　　shaken–taken

*111

THAT you were once unkind befriends me now,
　　And for that sorrow which I then did feel
Needs must I under my transgression bow,
Unless my nerves were brass or hammer'd steel.
For if you were by my unkindness shaken,
As I by yours, you've pass'd a hell of time ;
And I, a tyrant, have no leisure taken
To weigh how once I suffer'd in your crime.
O, that our night of woe might have remember'd
My deepest sense, how hard true sorrow hits,
And soon to you, as you to me then, tender'd
The humble salve which wounded bosoms fits !
　　But that your trespass now becomes a fee ;
　　Mine ransoms yours, and yours must ransom me.

shaken–taken　　　　　　　　　　　　(bow)

*112

YOUR love and pity doth the impression fill
    Which vulgar scandal stamp'd upon my brow ;
For what care I who calls me well or ill,
So you o'er-green my bad, my good allow ?
You are my all the world, and I must strive
To know my shames and praises from your tongue ;
None else to me, nor I to none alive,
That my steel'd sense or changes right or wrong.
In so profound abysm I throw all care
Of others' voices, that my adder's sense
To critic and to flatterer stopped are.
Mark how with my neglect I do dispense :
    You are so strongly in my purpose bred
    That all the world besides methinks are dead.

(brow)   (a)live

113

O, HOW thy worth with manners may I sing,
    When thou art all the better part of me ?
What can mine own praise to mine own self bring ?
And what is 't but mine own when I praise thee ?
Even for this let us divided live,
And our dear love lose name of single one,
That by this separation I may give
That due to thee which thou deserv'st alone.
O absence, what a torment wouldst thou prove,
Were it not thy sour leisure gave sweet leave
To entertain the time with thoughts of love,
Which time and thoughts so sweetly doth deceive,
    And that thou teachest how to make one twain,
    By praising him here who doth hence remain !

live   one–alone ; twain–remain
108 (*twain*)

114

L ET me confess that we two must be twain,
   Although our undivided loves are one ;
So shall those blots that do with me remain,
Without thy help, by me be borne alone.
In our two loves there is but one respect,
Though in our lives a separable spite,
Which though it alter not love's sole effect,
Yet doth it steal sweet hours from love's delight.
I may not evermore acknowledge thee,
Lest my bewailed guilt should do thee shame,
Nor thou with public kindness honour me,
Unless thou take that honour from thy name.
   But do not so ; I love thee in such sort,
   As thou being mine, mine is thy good report.

twain–remain ; one–alone   spite

115

T HEN hate me when thou wilt ; if ever, now ;
   Now, while the world is bent my deeds to cross,
Join with the spite of fortune, make me bow,
And do not drop in for an after-loss.
Ah, do not, when my heart hath 'scap'd this sorrow,
Come in the rearward of a conquer'd woe ;
Give not a windy night a rainy morrow,
To linger out a purpos'd overthrow.
If thou wilt leave me, do not leave me last,
When other petty griefs have done their spite,
But in the onset come : so shall I taste
At first the very worst of fortune's might ;
   And other strains of woe, which now seem woe,
   Compar'd with loss of thee will not seem so.

spite   woe

116

WHEN to the sessions of sweet silent thought
I summon up remembrance of things past,
I sigh the lack of many a thing I sought,
And with old woes new wail my dear time's waste;
Then can I drown an eye, unus'd to flow,
For precious friends hid in death's dateless night,
And weep afresh love's long since cancell'd woe,
And moan the expense of many a vanish'd sight;
Then can I grieve at grievances foregone,
And heavily from woe to woe tell o'er
The sad account of fore-bemoaned moan,
Which I new pay as if not paid before.
But if the while I think on thee, dear friend,
All losses are restor'd and sorrows end.

woe   (flow; moan)
                                  before; *end* 119

*117

THEY that have power to hurt and will do none,
That do not do the thing they most do show,
Who, moving others, are themselves as stone,
Unmoved, cold and to temptation slow;
They rightly do inherit heaven's graces
And husband nature's riches from expense;
They are the lords and owners of their faces,
Others but stewards of their excellence.
The summer's flower is to the summer sweet,
Though to itself it only live and die,
But if that flower with base infection meet,
The basest weed outbraves his dignity:
For sweetest things turn sourest by their deeds;
Lilies that fester smell far worse than weeds.

(slow; stone)   deeds

*118

O, FOR my sake do you with Fortune chide,
  The guilty goddess of my harmful deeds,
That did not better for my life provide
Than public means which public manners breeds.
Thence comes it that my name receives a brand,
And almost thence my nature is subdu'd
To what it works in, like the dyer's hand.
Pity me then and wish I were renew'd;
Whilst, like a willing patient, I will drink
Potions of eisel 'gainst my strong infection;
No bitterness that I will bitter think,
Nor double penance, to correct correction.
  Pity me then, dear friend, and I assure ye
  Even that your pity is enough to cure me.

deeds   hand

119

L IKE as the waves make towards the pebbled
    shore,
So do our minutes hasten to their end;
Each changing place with that which goes before,
In sequent toil all forwards do contend.
Nativity, once in the main of light,
Crawls to maturity, wherewith being crown'd,
Crooked eclipses 'gainst his glory fight,
And Time that gave doth now his gift confound.
Time doth transfix the flourish set on youth
And delves the parallels in beauty's brow,
Feeds on the rarities of nature's truth,
And nothing stands but for his scythe to mow.
  And yet to times in hope my verse shall stand,
  Praising thy worth, despite his cruel hand.

hand   shore
116 *end–before*   *youth–truth* 121

*120

WHEN I have seen by Time's fell hand defac'd
    The rich-proud cost of outworn buried age;
When sometime lofty towers I see down-raz'd,
And brass eternal slave to mortal rage;
When I have seen the hungry ocean gain
Advantage on the kingdom of the shore
And the firm soil win of the watery main,
Increasing store with loss and loss with store;
When I have seen such interchange of state,
Or state itself confounded to decay;
Ruin hath taught me thus to ruminate,
That Time will come and take my love away.
  This thought is as a death, which cannot choose
  But weep to have that which it fears to lose.

shore   store

121

AS a decrepit father takes delight
    To see his active child do deeds of youth,
So I, made lame by fortune's dearest spite,
Take all my comfort of thy worth and truth.
For whether beauty, birth, or wealth, or wit,
Or any of these all, or all, or more,
Entitled in thy parts do crowned sit,
I make my love engrafted to this store.
So then I am not lame, poor, nor despis'd,
Whilst that this shadow doth such substance give
That I in thy abundance am suffic'd
And by a part of all thy glory live.
Look, what is best, that best I wish in thee;
This wish I have; then ten times happy me!

store   youth–truth
119 *youth–truth*

122

ALAS, 'tis true I have gone here and there,
And made myself a motley to the view,
Gor'd mine own thoughts, sold cheap what is most
dear,
Made old offences of affections new ;
Most true it is that I have look'd on truth
Askance and strangely : but, by all above,
These blenches gave my heart another youth,
And worse essays prov'd thee my best of love !
Now all is done, have what shall have no end !
Mine appetite I never more will grind
On newer proof, to try an older friend,
A god in love, to whom I am confin'd.
　　Then give me welcome, next my heaven the best,
　　Even to thy pure and most most loving breast.

truth–youth　　　　　　　　　　　　　　　　new
　　　　　　　　　　　　　　　　　　　(best) 125

*123

WHAT potions have I drunk of Siren tears,
Distill'd from limbecks foul as hell within,
Applying fears to hopes and hopes to fears,
Still losing when I saw myself to win !
What wretched errors hath my heart committed,
Whilst it hath thought itself so blessed never !
How have mine eyes out of their spheres been fitted,
In the distraction of this madding fever !
O benefit of ill ! now I find true
That better is by evil still made better ;
And ruin'd love, when it is built anew,
Grows fairer than at first, more strong, far greater.
　　So I return rebuk'd to my content,
　　And gain by ills thrice more than I have spent.

(a)new　　　　　　　　　　　　　　　　　　true

*124

L IKE as, to make our appetites more keen,
    With eager compounds we our palate urge ;
As, to prevent our maladies unseen,
We sicken to shun sickness when we purge ;
Even so, being full of your ne'er-cloying sweetness,
To bitter sauces did I frame my feeding ;
And sick of welfare found a kind of meetness
To be diseas'd, ere that there was true needing.
Thus policy in love, to anticipate
The ills that were not, grew to faults assur'd,
And brought to medicine a healthful state,
Which, rank of goodness, would by ill be cur'd.
  But thence I learn, and find the lesson true,
  Drugs poison him that so fell sick of you.

true   state

125

W HEN, in disgrace with fortune and men's eyes,
    I all alone beweep my outcast state,
And trouble deaf heaven with my bootless cries,
And look upon myself, and curse my fate,
Wishing me like to one more rich in hope,
Featur'd like him, like him with friends possess'd,
Desiring this man's art and that man's scope,
With what I most enjoy contented least ;
Yet in these thoughts myself almost despising,
Haply I think on thee, and then my state,
Like to the lark at break of day arising
From sullen earth, sings hymns at heaven's gate ;
  For thy sweet love remember'd such wealth brings
  That then I scorn to change my state with kings.

state   (state)
122 (*possess'd*)

126

FAREWELL ! thou art too dear for my possessing,
  And like enough thou know'st thy estimate :
The charter of thy worth gives thee releasing ;
My bonds in thee are all determinate.
For how do I hold thee but by thy granting ?
And for that riches where is my deserving ?
The cause of this fair gift in me is wanting,
And so my patent back again is swerving.
Thyself thou gav'st, thy own worth then not knowing,
Or me, to whom thou gav'st it, else mistaking ;
So thy great gift, upon misprision growing,
Comes home again, on better judgment making.
  Thus have I had thee, as a dream doth flatter,
  In sleep a king, but waking no such matter.

(estimate)   (determinate)
                                        (*determinate*) 128

PART II

*127

THOSE lips that Love's own hand did make
  Breath'd forth the sound that said ' I hate,'
To me that languish'd for her sake.
But when she saw my woeful state,
Straight in her heart did mercy come,
Chiding that tongue that ever sweet
Was us'd in giving gentle doom ;
And taught it thus anew to greet :
' I hate ' she alter'd with an end,
That follow'd it as gentle day
Doth follow night, who, like a fiend,
From heaven to hell is flown away ;
  ' I hate ' from hate away she threw,
  And sav'd my life, saying ' not you.'

(state)   state

128

HOW oft, when thou, my music, music play'st,
    Upon that blessed wood whose motion sounds
With thy sweet fingers, when thou gently sway'st
The wiry concord that mine ear confounds,
Do I envy those jacks that nimble leap
To kiss the tender inward of thy hand,
Whilst my poor lips, which should that harvest reap,
At the wood's boldness by thee blushing stand!
To be so tickled, they would change their state
And situation with those dancing chips,
O'er whom thy fingers walk with gentle gait,
Making dead wood more blest than living lips.
  Since saucy jacks so happy are in this,
  Give them thy fingers, me thy lips to kiss.

state   hand
126 (*state*)   (*kiss*) 130

129

THE little Love-god lying once asleep
    Laid by his side his heart-inflaming brand,
Whilst many nymphs that vow'd chaste life to keep
Came tripping by. But in her maiden hand
The fairest votary took up that fire
Which many legions of true hearts had warm'd.
And so the general of hot desire
Was sleeping by a virgin hand disarm'd.
This brand she quenched in a cool well by,
Which from Love's fire took heat perpetual,
Growing a bath and healthful remedy
For men diseas'd. But I, my mistress' thrall,
  Came there for cure, and this by that I prove :
  Love's fire heats water, water cools not love.

hand   prove–love

130

L OVE is too young to know what conscience is ;
Yet who knows not conscience is born of love ?
Then, gentle cheater, urge not my amiss,
Lest guilty of my faults thy sweet self prove.
For, thou betraying me, I do betray
My nobler part to my gross body's treason.
My soul doth tell my body that he may
Triumph in love ; flesh stays no farther reason,
But rising at thy name doth point out thee
As his triumphant prize. Proud of this pride,
He is contented thy poor drudge to be,
To stand in thy affairs, fall by thy side.
 No want of conscience hold it that I call
 Her ' love ' for whose dear love I rise and fall.

love–prove   love–prove
128 (*amiss*)

131

I F thy soul check thee that I come so near,
Swear to thy blind soul that I was thy ' Will,'
And will, thy soul knows, is admitted there ;
Thus far for love, my love-suit, sweet, fulfil.
' Will ' will fulfil the treasure of thy love,
Ay, fill it full with wills, and my will one.
In things of great receipt with ease we prove
Among a number one is reckon'd none.
Then in the number let me pass untold,
Though in thy store's account I one must be ;
For nothing hold me, so it please thee hold
That nothing me, a something sweet to thee.
 Make but my name thy love, and love that still,
 And then thou lovest me, for my name is ' Will.'

love–prove   Will–still

132

WHOEVER hath her wish, thou hast thy ' Will,'
  And ' Will ' to boot, and ' Will ' in overplus ;
More than enough am I that vex thee still,
To thy sweet will making addition thus.
Wilt thou, whose will is large and spacious,
Not once vouchsafe to hide my will in thine ?
Shall will in others seem right gracious,
And in my will no fair acceptance shine ?
The sea, all water, yet receives rain still,
And in abundance addeth to his store ;
So thou, being rich in ' Will,' add to thy ' Will '
One will of mine, to make thy large ' Will ' more.
  Let no unkind No fair beseechers kill ;
    Think all but one, and me in that one ' Will.'

Will–still   Will–still

133

LO, as a careful housewife runs to catch
  One of her feather'd creatures broke away,
Sets down her babe, and makes all swift dispatch
In pursuit of the thing she would have stay ;
Whilst her neglected child holds her in chase,
Cries to catch her whose busy care is bent
To follow that which flies before her face,
Not prizing her poor infant's discontent :
So runn'st thou after that which flies from thee,
Whilst I, thy babe, chase thee afar behind.
But if thou catch thy hope, turn back to me,
And play the mother's part, kiss me, be kind ;
  So will I pray that thou mayst have thy ' Will,'
    If thou turn back and my loud crying still.

Will–still   Will–still ; kind

134

SO now I have confess'd that he is thine,
  And I myself am mortgag'd to thy will.
Myself I'll forfeit, so that other mine
Thou wilt restore, to be my comfort still.
But thou wilt not, nor he will not be free,
For thou art covetous and he is kind ;
He learn'd but surety-like to write for me,
Under that bond that him as fast doth bind.
The statute of thy beauty thou wilt take,
Thou usurer, that put'st forth all to use,
And sue a friend came debtor for my sake ;
So him I lose through my unkind abuse.
  Him have I lost ; thou hast both him and me ;
  He pays the whole, and yet am I not free.

Will–still ; kind   (free)

135

BESHREW that heart that makes my heart to
  groan
For that deep wound it gives my friend and me !
Is't not enough to torture me alone,
But slave to slavery my sweet'st friend must be ?
Me from myself thy cruel eye hath taken,
And my next self thou harder hast engross'd ;
Of him, myself, and thee, I am forsaken ;
A torment thrice threefold thus to be cross'd.
But then my friend's heart let my poor heart bail ;
Whoe'er keeps me, let my heart be his guard ;
Thou canst not then use rigour in my gaol.
  And yet thou wilt ; for I, being pent in thee,
  Perforce am thine, and all that is in me.

(be)   (be ; cross'd)

136

IN loving thee thou know'st I am forsworn,
  But thou art twice forsworn, to me love swearing ;
In act thy bed-vow broke, and new faith torn,
In vowing new hate after new love bearing.
But why of two oaths' breach do I accuse thee,
When I break twenty ! I am perjur'd most :
For all my vows are oaths but to misuse thee,
And all my honest faith in thee is lost ;
For I have sworn deep oaths of thy deep kindness,
Oaths of thy love, thy truth, thy constancy ;
And, to enlighten thee, gave eyes to blindness,
Or made them swear against the thing they see ;
  For I have sworn thee fair ; more perjur'd I,
  To swear against the truth so foul a lie !

(lost ; see)   (see)

137

LOVE is my sin, and thy dear virtue hate,
  Hate of my sin, grounded on sinful loving.
O, but with mine compare thou thine own state,
And thou shalt find it merits not reproving ;
Or if it do, not from those lips of thine,
That have profan'd their scarlet ornaments
And seal'd false bonds of love, as oft as mine
Robb'd others' beds' revenues of their rents.
Be it lawful I love thee, as thou lov'st those
Whom thine eyes woo as mine importune thee ;
Root pity in thy heart, that, when it grows,
Thy pity may deserve to pitied be.
  If thou dost seek to have what thou dost hide,
  By self-example mayst thou be denied !

(be)   (hide)

9

138

BE wise as thou art cruel; do not press
    My tongue-tied patience with too much disdain;
Lest sorrow lend me words, and words express
The manner of my pity-wanting pain.
If I might teach thee wit, better it were,
Though not to love, yet, love, to tell me so;
As testy sick men, when their deaths be near,
No news but health from their physicians know.
For, if I should despair, I should grow mad,
And in my madness might speak ill of thee;
Now this ill-wresting world is grown so bad,
Mad slanderers by mad ears believed be.
    That I may not be so, nor thou belied,
      Bear thine eyes straight, though thy proud heart
        go wide.

(wide)   disdain–pain

139

THINE eyes I love, and they, as pitying me,
    Knowing thy heart torments me with disdain,
Have put on black and loving mourners be,
Looking with pretty ruth upon my pain.
And truly not the morning sun of heaven
Better becomes the grey cheeks of the east,
Nor that full star that ushers in the even
Doth half that glory to the sober west,
As those two mourning eyes become thy face.
O, let it then as well beseem thy heart
To mourn for me, since mourning doth thee grace,
And suit thy pity like in every part.
    Then will I swear beauty herself is black,
      And all they foul that thy complexion lack.

disdain–pain   face–grace;   black–lack
                                           face 141

*140

IN the old age black was not counted fair;
　Or if it were, it bore not beauty's name.
But now is black beauty's successive heir,
And beauty slander'd with a bastard shame.
For since each hand hath put on nature's power,
Fairing the foul with art's false borrow'd face,
Sweet beauty hath no name, no holy bower,
But is profan'd, if not lives in disgrace.
Therefore my mistress' hairs are raven black,
Her eyes so suited, and they mourners seem
At such who, not born fair, no beauty lack,
Slandering creation with a false esteem.
　　Yet so they mourn, becoming of their woe,
　　That every tongue says beauty should look so.

face–(dis)grace ;　black–lack   face

141

THOU art as tyrannous, so as thou art,
　　As those whose beauties proudly make them
　　cruel ;
For well thou know'st to my dear doting heart
Thou art the fairest and most precious jewel.
Yet in good faith some say that thee behold,
Thy face hath not the power to make love groan.
To say they err I dare not be so bold,
Although I swear it to myself alone.
And to be sure that is not false I swear,
A thousand groans, but thinking on thy face,
One on another's neck, do witness bear
Thy black is fairest in my judgment's place.
　　In nothing art thou black save in thy deeds,
　　And thence this slander, as I think, proceeds.

face   alone
139 face

142

IN faith, I do not love thee with mine eyes,
   For they in thee a thousand errors note ;
But 'tis my heart that loves what they despise,
Who, in despite of view, is pleas'd to dote ;
Nor are mine ears with thy tongue's tune delighted ;
Nor tender feeling to base touches prone,
Nor taste, nor smell, desire to be invited
To any sensual feast with thee alone ;
But my five wits nor my five senses can
Dissuade one foolish heart from serving thee,
Who leaves unsway'd the likeness of a man,
Thy proud heart's slave and vassal wretch to be.
   Only my plague thus far I count my gain,
   That she that makes me sin awards me pain.

alone   eyes
                                              pain 145

*143

THOU blind fool, Love, what dost thou to mine
      eyes,
That they behold, and see not what they see ?
They know what beauty is, see where it lies,
Yet what the best is take the worst to be.
If eyes, corrupt by over-partial looks,
Be anchor'd in the bay where all men ride,
Why of eye's falsehood hast thou forged hooks,
Whereto the judgment of my heart is tied ?
Why should my heart think that a several plot
Which my heart knows the wide world's common
      place ?
Or mine eyes seeing this, say this is not,
To put fair truth upon so foul a face ?
   In things right true my heart and eyes have err'd,
   And to this false plague are they now transferr'd.

eyes   lies

*144

WHEN my love swears that she is made of truth,
  I do believe her, though I know she lies,
That she might think me some untutor'd youth,
Unlearned in the world's false subtleties.
Thus vainly thinking that she thinks me young,
Although she knows my days are past the best,
Simply I credit her false-speaking tongue ;
On both sides thus is simple truth suppress'd.
But wherefore says she not she is unjust ?
And wherefore say not I that I am old ?
O, love's best habit is in seeming trust,
And age in love loves not to have years told.
  Therefore I lie with her and she with me,
  And in our faults by lies we flatter'd be.

lies   tongue

145

O CALL not me to justify the wrong
  That thy unkindness lays upon my heart.
Wound me not with thine eye, but with thy tongue ;
Use power with power, and slay me not by art.
Tell me thou lov'st elsewhere ; but in my sight,
Dear heart, forbear to glance thine eye aside.
What need'st thou wound with cunning, when thy
      might
Is more than my o'er-press'd defence can bide ?
Let me excuse thee : ah, my love well knows
Her pretty looks have been mine enemies ;
And therefore from my face she turns my foes,
That they elsewhere might dart their injuries.
  Yet do not so ; but since I am near slain,
  Kill me outright with looks, and rid my pain.

tongue   (enemies)
142 *pain*

146

CANST thou, O cruel! say I love thee not,
    When I against myself with thee partake?
Do I not think on thee, when I forgot
Am of myself, all-tyrant, for thy sake?
Who hateth thee that I do call my friend?
On whom frown'st thou that I do fawn upon?
Nay, if thou lour'st on me, do I not spend
Revenge upon myself with present moan?
What merit do I in myself respect,
That is so proud thy service to despise,
When all my best doth worship thy defect,
Commanded by the motion of thine eyes?
  But, love, hate on, for now I know thy mind:
  Those that can see thou lov'st, and I am blind.

(despise)   eyes
                                           blind 149

*147

CUPID laid by his brand and fell asleep.
    A maid of Dian's this advantage found,
And his love-kindling fire did quickly steep
In a cold valley-fountain of that ground;
Which borrow'd from this holy fire of Love
A dateless lively heat, still to endure,
And grew a seething bath, which yet men prove
Against strange maladies a sovereign cure.
But at my mistress' eye Love's brand new-fir'd,
The boy for trial needs would touch my breast;
I, sick withal, the help of bath desir'd,
And thither hied, a sad distemper'd guest,
  But found no cure. The bath for my help lies
  Where Cupid got new fire: my mistress' eyes.

eyes   ground

*148

MY mistress' eyes are nothing like the sun;
  Coral is far more red than her lips' red:
If snow be white, why then her breasts are dun;
If hairs be wires, black wires grow on her head.
I have seen roses damask'd, red and white,
But no such roses see I in her cheeks;
And in some perfumes is there more delight
Than in the breath that from my mistress reeks.
I love to hear her speak, yet well I know
That music hath a far more pleasing sound;
I grant I never saw a goddess go,
My mistress, when she walks, treads on the ground:
  And yet, by heaven, I think my love as rare
  As any she belied with false compare.

ground   (white; go)

149

O ME! what eyes hath Love put in my head,
  Which have no correspondence with true sight!
Or, if they have, where is my judgment fled,
That censures falsely what they see aright?
If that be fair whereon my false eyes dote,
What means the world to say it is not so?
If it be not, then love doth well denote
Love's eye is not so true as all men's. No,
How can it? O, how can Love's eye be true,
That is so vex'd with watching and with tears?
No marvel then, though I mistake my view;
The sun itself sees not till heaven clears.
  O cunning love! with tears thou keep'st me blind,
  Lest eyes well-seeing thy foul faults should find.

(sight; so)   (sight)
146 *blind*

150

MY love is as a fever, longing still
  For that which longer nurseth the disease;
Feeding on that which doth preserve the ill,
The uncertain sickly appetite to please.
My reason, the physician to my love,
Angry that his prescriptions are not kept,
Hath left me, and I desperate now approve,
Desire is death, which physic did except.
Past cure I am, now reason is past care,
And frantic-mad with evermore unrest;
My thoughts and my discourse as madmen's are,
At random from the truth vainly express'd.
  For I have sworn thee fair, and thought thee bright,
  Who art as black as hell, as dark as night!

(night)   ill

151

O, FROM what power hast thou this powerful
     might
With insufficiency my heart to sway?
To make me give the lie to my true sight,
And swear that brightness doth not grace the day?
Whence hast thou this becoming of things ill,
That in the very refuse of thy deeds
There is such strength and warrantise of skill,
That, in my mind, thy worst all best exceeds?
Who taught thee how to make me love thee more,
The more I hear and see just cause of hate?
O, though I love what others do abhor,
With others thou shouldst not abhor my state.
  If thy unworthiness rais'd love in me,
  More worthy I to be belov'd of thee.

ill   (state)

152

THE expense of spirit in a waste of shame
   Is lust in action ; and till action, lust
Is perjur'd, murderous, bloody, full of blame,
Savage, extreme, rude, cruel, not to trust ;
Enjoy'd no sooner but despised straight ;
Past reason hunted ; and no sooner had,
Past reason hated, as a swallow'd bait,
On purpose laid to make the taker mad ;
Mad in pursuit, and in possession so ;
Had, having, and in quest to have, extreme ;
A bliss in proof, and prov'd, a very woe ;
Before, a joy propos'd ; behind, a dream.
  All this the world well knows ; yet none knows well
  To shun the heaven that leads men to this hell.

(bait)   hell

*153

TWO loves I have of comfort and despair,
   Which like two spirits do suggest me still :
The better angel is a man right fair,
The worser spirit a woman colour'd ill.
To win me soon to hell, my female evil
Tempteth my better angel from my side,
And would corrupt my saint to be a devil,
Wooing his purity with her foul pride.
And whether that my angel be turn'd fiend
Suspect I may, yet not directly tell ;
But being both from me, both to each friend,
I guess one angel in another's hell.
  Yet this shall I ne'er know, but live in doubt,
  Till my bad angel fire my good one out.

hell   (friend)

*154

POOR soul, the centre of my sinful earth,
  Rebuke these rebel powers that thee array;
Why dost thou pine within and suffer dearth,
Painting thy outward walls so costly gay?
Why so large cost, having so short a lease,
Dost thou upon thy fading mansion spend?
Shall worms, inheritors of this excess,
Eat up thy charge? is this thy body's end?
Then, soul, live thou upon thy servant's loss,
And let that pine to aggravate thy store;
Buy terms divine in selling hours of dross;
Within be fed, without be rich no more.
  So shalt thou feed on Death, that feeds on men;
  And Death once dead, there's no more dying then.

(end)

NOTES

1. l. 7. So Beeching: Quarto " A man in hue " which can hardly be wrested to sense. Cf. Merchant of Venice II vii, " What says the silver with her virgin hue ? "

28. ll. 5–6. The only instance (for 88, in which an allegorical *thou* appears in a *you-sonnet*, is none) of a change in the pronoun of address from *thou* to *you* within a sonnet. Dowden suggests that *you* and *your* may be used indefinitely ; but though this might hold in line 5, *your true image* must surely be definite. The explanation may be carelessness in revision or possibly a mere copyist error.

35. l. 11. So G. C. M. Smith ; Quarto *naigh noe dull flesh* ; most editors *neigh—no dull flesh—*, which is questionable natural history ; un-Shakespearean (though good Browning) in style ; and leaves *But* in the next line in the air. Smith explains : desire will decline to be a burden on the horse's back. Much better take *weigh* in the common Shakespearean meaning of care for, trouble about.

55. l. 3. Quarto *Reserve their character*. Editors *preserve their ; rehearse thy, your, their ; reserve thy, your ; deserve their ; rescribe their ; receive thy ;* etc. As line 1 implies *I think good thoughts*, lines 2–3 ought according to 5 to mean *while other write good words*. Hence one would expect ' comments of your praise are charactered ' (i.e. written down) ; or rather ' others character comments of your praise,' for the parallelism is active not passive throughout : ' other write good words ; afford hymns ; breathe words.' Hence the reading in the text. *Rehearse* is used four times in this group, 44, 46, 58 and 61 (where one is also tempted to substitute *rehearsing* for *of hearsay*, which all but defies honest interpretation).

125

63. l. 10. Quarto (and all editors but one) *thy deeds*. Confusion between *thy* and *their* in the Quarto is common. Thus the Quarto reads *their outward* for *thy outward* in line 5.

94. l. 11. Quarto *doth lye*. Many editors follow Malone in changing to *do lie*. The change, though tempting, would be hardly justified by Shakespearean usage if the sonnet stood alone. It becomes a certainty when the next sonnet with *do lie* in its first line is restored from its displacement in the Quarto to its proper place.

96. ll. 5–7. Quarto and all editors *accident, discontent*, cf. the note next following.

98. l. 1. Quarto *monument*. All editors but one *monuments*.

l. 4. Quarto *unswept stone*, which must apparently be explained as *besmear'd with sluttish time* ; Stengal *in swept stone*, which is another way of putting *marble*.

104. ll. 2–4. Quarto and all editors *defects, respects*. For *defect* cf. sonnet 146 *All my best doth worship thy defect*. For *respect* cf. King John IV ii. *More upon humour than advis'd respect*.

105. l. 14. So several modern editors, for the Quarto *maketh mine untrue*. Cf. *mine eye saith true* in 106, which carries on the argument.

INDEX OF FIRST LINES

(The Roman numerals give the Quarto order)

127

Printed in Great Britain by Butler & Tanner Ltd., Frome and London

CONCORDIA UNIVERSITY LIBRARY

3 9371 00052 0643

PR 2848 .A2 B7
Shakespeare, William, 1564-
1616.
The original order of